Praise for UNCOVERY

Amanda Jones's book is beautifully written and eminently readable. Her personal story of awakening is inspiring and points the reader in the direction of their true self. Amanda is a gifted storyteller, who shares an understanding that is simple yet profound. It provides hope for anyone who is looking for true and lasting transformation. Her candor and authenticity reveal deftly and intelligently how we don't need to be afraid of our humanness, and she provides real world examples that show the path to healing is much easier than we think. Read this book and be impacted by the wisdom of Amanda's heart. – Rohini Ross MA, LMFT

Psychotherapist

Best-selling author of Marriage — (Soul-Centered Series Book 1)

Uncovery by Amanda Jones is an incredibly honest, thought provoking tangible gift for anyone out there who believes they are not enough. This book smashes the view many have about the source and the sustainability of their mental health and invites readers to take a fresh and transformational view of how they create their experience of life. Uncovery truly uncovers how our minds work practically and pragmatically through Amanda's insightful writing and her wonderfully colorful character.

Read it now.... you will not be disappointed!

Jacquie Forde RGN, RM

Principles Coach and Leadership Consultant, CEO The Wellbeing Academy

UNCOVERY

A NEW UNDERSTANDING BEHIND RADICAL
FREEDOM FROM EATING DISORDERS
AND DEPRESSION

AMANDA JONES

Cover design by Sandra Koenig
Edited by Mary Schiller
Foreword edited by Rachel Blackmon
Author photograph ©Leandra Blei

Uncovery/ Amanda Jones —1st ed.
ISBN 978-1981193028

Contents

This book is dedicated to you.

"Where something becomes extremely difficult and unbearable, there we also stand already quite near its transformation."

— Rainer Maria Rilke

Happiness hit her like a bullet in the back...

Dog Days Are Over

Florence + The Machine

FOREWORD

Imagine there is a river running through you.

Your entire experience of life flows through you, down that river. Everything you think, feel, and do passes through, powered by the current of the river.

Your emotions, your opinions, your sense of identity ... your habits, diagnoses, and choices ... they aren't still or solid, sitting somewhere. They are brought to life, felt, and then they drift away. They are in constant motion, naturally replaced with a revolving stream of new experience.

You aren't responsible for what flows down the river.

The particular thoughts and feelings that show up aren't yours. You didn't put them there and, in most cases, you didn't choose them. They are simply part of the flow of life.

Your thoughts and feelings don't come from the world outside the river; they can't. What flows down the river is born of the river. What that means, in human terms (since this is a metaphor for how human life works, after all), is that what you feel originates within you. Life out there—your relationships, job, body, health, or any circumstance at all—cannot create or dictate your experience. Your experience begins and ends within you.

You (what you call me) are not the contents of the river. You are what remains when all has passed through. The contents of the river are in perpetual flux. You are what never changes.

It's an incredible design! Can you get a feel for who you are? For the fleeting and safe nature of your experience?

You are awareness of life itself. The things you witness don't stick. This means there is nothing to avoid, fear, change, or chase away. The current takes care of that for you, endlessly updating your experience in each and every moment.

If this is an accurate metaphor for human life, why do we feel so stuck at times? Why does our experience look so repetitive, and why do our issues appear to linger and weigh us down?

It's simple: we misunderstand the design.

No one told you life worked this way, so you identify with and latch onto what flows down the river. You say things like I had this thought. I don't like this feeling. I should be different. I can't believe I did/said/ate that.

It's happening within you, after all.

You—like all people—miss the fact that your experience isn't you. It isn't serious. It's life taking temporary form, expressing itself through you. Then flowing downstream making way for new and different temporary expressions.

Your wellbeing and your essential nature are ultimately unaffected by what washes over you. But when you don't realize that, you innocently get in the way of the natural flow. We all do.

When what's flowing through you looks personal and stable, of course you try to fix or change it. You jump in the river that is flowing and recycling perfectly on its own. You stand in the flow with your bucket, scooping up water that was trying to flow downstream. You carry that bucket around, showing everyone proof of your problems.

"See!" you say. "It's right here in my bucket!" You replay what you did yesterday and fixate on fears and worries about what will happen tomorrow. When it looks like life out there can hurt us, or like what flows through us can hurt us, we're filled with anxiety about what might show up next. Then we wonder why change is so hard.

"There must be a problem with me", we conclude. We're broken. There is a problem in our design.

But make no mistake—you and the design of life are perfect. The only problem is your innocent misunderstanding of the source of your experience. The innocent misunderstanding (shared with virtually everyone on earth) of how the river operates.

Seeing through these misunderstandings is the purpose of this book. When people catch a glimpse of the resilient, health-affirming design of life, they uncover the wellbeing that has always been there.

It no longer makes sense to say that you "have" a disorder or habit. You experience thoughts, feelings, and behaviors but they don't have to linger or leave a mark. They aren't personal.

Amanda was furiously treading water in the river when I first met her. Everything looked important, personal, and meaningful. What she ate, when she ate, how life appeared within and around her.

Only a few short years before I met Amanda, I was there myself— trying to keep from drowning in my own anxieties and eating habits. Amanda and I didn't realize that life as we knew it was being created within us, moment to moment. Life wasn't happening to us. We weren't feeling the effects of our past or our weight or some mental flaw we possessed.

We didn't realize it was possible to watch the river from its banks. That our experience didn't brand us with diagnoses and labels that meant something deep or stable about us.

Labels and diagnoses describe some of the thoughts and behaviors we experienced at particular points in time, from particular states of mind. They described the contents of any given bucket of water taken from the river.

But fresh, new water is always coming. There is nothing to fix.

As Amanda and I (and many, many people we've talked with) explored the Principles behind life that you're going to read about, we noticed one day that life felt lighter. We were no longer carrying buckets around.

We became naturally less tangled in the flow of life. The past—whether it's five years or five seconds ago—does not exist. It's amazing how much easier life flows when you aren't taking stock of the past or preparing for the future. When you aren't trying to control or change what shows up.

There is enormous hope for everyone—our incredible design ensures it! Anything that burdens you can wash away to reveal the health and wellbeing that is within you right now.

Uncovered.

Amy Johnson, Ph.D.

January 24, 2018

❧

Introduction

Why Uncovery?

> *The cosmos is within us. We are made of star-stuff. We are a way for the universe to know itself.*
>
> —*Carl Sagan*

In October of 2016, I eagerly boarded a plane bound for Los Angeles, California. I was headed to a conference presented by the Three Principles Global Community, a worldwide non-profit dedicated to spreading education and awareness of the Three Principles understanding.

My flight arrived and I joined the throngs of LA commuters in a slow crawl, ninety-minute commute to the hotel venue. I was filled with anticipation and excitement because I was about to spend a weekend with people that I had only previously worked with and learned from over an internet connection.

I never had an inclination to attend a conference of any sort in the past. But deciding to attend this one was a no-brainer: the understanding that was the focus of this conference had completely and irrevocably changed my life.

I hastily checked into my room and rushed down to the registration table to pick up my badge and program, eyes scanning the vicinity for familiar faces. There was a cocktail reception and gathering in the courtyard, where I wandered out into the balmy candlelit evening equipped with a hefty dose of nervous excitement, feeling like a child slipping in unnoticed while the grown-ups mingled.

I spotted the champagne bar and headed directly for it, trying to maintain an air of poise and *stay cool*, but was pretty sure the I-can't-believe-how-far-I've-come-I-never-would-have-guessed-it smile cemented on my face was unmistakable.

Champagne in hand, I pulled myself together and sought out a few familiar faces.

The evening progressed, the champagne flowed and I connected with several very special people who would later become close friends and colleagues.

As the evening began to wind down, I was talking with a woman who asked how I came to be at the conference. I gave her a quick synopsis and she introduced herself as Jeanne Catherine Gray, the host of a podcast radio show called *Waking Up: The Neuroscience of Awareness*. I had been a listener and fan of the show, and as we continued to talk I found her to be as delightful and genuine in person as she was on the air. After listening to my story, she invited me to be a guest on the show. I was taken aback and asked her why she would want to interview me; I wasn't really sure what I could offer. (I figured there were better stories out there, not yet fully grasping the scope of what I had discovered in this understanding that I write about in this book.) She graciously explained that my experience in finding lasting freedom from eating disorders and depression after 23 years was something people would find inspiring and helpful, not to mention a perfect case study of success outside the traditional psychotherapy paradigm. Really?

I immediately accepted her offer, while simultaneously feeling a bit befuddled from the fact that I had *never* talked about my experience in such an open and unguarded way before, let alone on the radio.

I floated up to my room at the end of the night on a cloud of blissful joy and reflected on the events of the evening. I realized that I really *did* want to share my story and, more importantly, share what I discovered that led me out of decades of bulimia, anorexia, and depression. Not to share that I recovered by getting lucky, or by listening to the right therapist or by seeing even that I was anyone special. I didn't possess any unusual amount of superhuman willpower or mental toughness to beat down my unwanted behaviors and diagnoses. On the contrary, I spent over two decades engaged in various attempts at traditional cognitive behavioral therapies. I immersed myself in meditation, yoga, and positive thinking strategies. I repeated daily affirmations, I journaled, I stuck post-it notes scribbled with inspirational quotes on every mirror. I tried everything that promised freedom and change.

I was told again and again by loving and well-meaning therapists that eating disorders and depression would be hard to recover from and that those conditions would always be with me in some capacity, as if I had been dealt a faulty set of cards to forever shuffle around. I was even told once that the average time for recovery was 10 years, and the best I could do was learn to cope with it. To say I was discouraged would be an understatement.

So what made my transformation worthy of sharing?

I came across an understanding that rendered willpower and mental toughness -- what are widely accepted as required -- traits completely unnecessary. Really.

A few days later, Jeanne Catherine asked me if I had an idea for a title for my interview. "Recovery from an Eating Disorder" didn't sound quite right, though I wasn't sure why: that *is* what happened, right?

I sat with it for a while, having discovered that answers bubble up when I get out of the way. Then it came to me. *Recovery* was not the right word at all. I hadn't re-covered anything. I had *uncovered* the innate, untouched well-being and peace that was always there.

Boom.

It would be a gross understatement to say that I never thought I would be where I am today: sharing what I've seen within this new paradigm of psychology. I never thought I would be well enough to help others. I didn't believe that there was something fundamental that I could share and thus would apply to everyone, regardless of their circumstances. I now speak with people around the world who are struggling to find their way out of eating disorders, anxiety, depression and unwanted habits.

I get to watch their lives transform with an understanding that requires no steps or strategies, an understanding that is sweeping the globe and quite literally changing lives.

My intention is not to write a self-help book; rather I want to point you in a different direction – toward that Self that needs no help, no fixing, no changing, the innate health and resilience that lies within every one of us, even when we can't imagine anything of the sort. I want to point you toward an understanding that unfolds within you and directs you to the fact and experience of this innate well-being.

You have everything you need to know already; it's just be
and re-covered. You are not an exception.

If you are suffering with an eating disorder (or any other habit), anxiety, or depression, this book may be very different from what you
might expect. I have no steps, plans or practices to give you. When
we are suffering, it is common and somewhat comforting to seek out
the next new strategy to free ourselves, once and for all. I am here to
tell you that not only do those things ultimately fail us, but the freedom you seek is *profoundly* more simple and close by than you have
been led to believe.

Really.

These truths have been pointed to and suggested by way of the
phrase *"look within"* for millennia through a myriad of wise teachings.
It just happens that this particularly unshrouded way of understanding our true source of experience has hit home faster and clearer than
any other teaching or philosophy that attempts to explain and decipher the human experience.

The good news is that there is nothing to *do*, only more to understand, to uncover. It really is that simple.

To get the most out of what I am attempting to point to in this book, I
gently suggest you read from an open mind. In other words, as you
read through the book, try to resist comparing this understanding and
the insights that show up for you with what you may have already
learned, researched, or studied. It will be helpful to read slowly and
not jump ahead. You will hear things repeated; this is intentional and
helps to build a foundation conducive to insight. I will be using certain words in italics and bold type to draw attention and point to a
deeper meaning beyond those particular words.

When I first came across this understanding, I immediately collated the similarities in my mind with past philosophies and teachings. I quickly learned that doing this only served to feed my intellect and add to my data storage to pull from when needed, but did not serve to penetrate any deeper than *"another good idea"* and *"yeah, I've heard this before"*.

It took a bit of unlearning to clear my slate and be able to see with unconditioned eyes what was being pointed to, and furthermore that there actually *was* something being pointed to.

The underlying message is pointing toward a feeling: a deeper, more profound place of understanding than what mere words can sufficiently portray. A *knowing,* in the way that you know your own name. Imagine how you listen to music or gaze upon a work of art; the words themselves are single brush strokes meant to create and evoke a deeper meaning and a much larger picture. Sense what sounds true to *you* on a level beneath the commentary in your head.

My journey began years ago, but as you will come to see later, the past is irrelevant to the possibility and enormity of transformation in the present. My childhood and upbringing was incredibly loving and supportive. My parents sacrificed for and encouraged my sister and me to the fullest and still do to this day. I am incredibly grateful. They gave us every opportunity to flourish and have been with me throughout this journey with nothing but love.

I will share a bit of my early experience to provide context as to where I am coming from and how I came to see what was previously invisible and covered over –- what was hidden behind the wizard's curtain.

❧

ONE

The Road to Oz

Pay no attention to that man behind the

curtain!

-The Wizard of Oz

I'm nine years old, perched on the floor in front of our television set in Seattle, Washington, flipping through channels when I suddenly come across a filmed production of American Ballet Theatre's *Nutcracker Ballet*. I am mesmerized. I had seen dance before, but for some reason at this moment in our living room I feel like I am watching something for the first time.

I experience a feeling of indescribable connection and longing that surpassed any passing curiosity that previous exposure to dance provided. I remember being drawn in by the other-worldly bodies defying gravity. My young mind and heart were engrossed, and I desperately wanted to be as magical and remarkable as those beings on stage. I felt for the first time what I recognize now was a sense of direction and purpose: I was going to be a dancer.

I didn't know how or when, or even if I could do it, but there was no question that an impression was left on me that afternoon, and I was going to pursue it. With the full support of my parents, my dance training began at age 10, and I was off on a focused and dedicated path. I felt enormous peace and joy when I was dancing, and I innocently super-glued my well-being and self-worth to dance: to being a dancer and looking like a dancer. Innocent. That point needs to be made clearly; it was completely **real** to me that the good feelings I was having were directly connected to, and *were a result of,* my chosen passion. It never occurred to me that this connection was not real. Why would it?

Between the ages of 10 and 12, I wasn't yet comparing myself to others and believing myself to be less than good enough. I felt unbridled freedom in movement and expression. I remember learning a phrase of choreography and dropping into a blissful lightness and flow. It made me happy. I wanted to do more of what made me happy. It was in this early infatuation that I began to construct my self-image within rigid walls of conformity to a mental concept of what it took to be worthy. Innocently. As I matured through the pre-teen years, I became more focused on the appearance and shape of my body as a dancer and what that image should look like in my mind. I began to compare myself to other dancers. Scrutiny of my body and comparing myself to others became instinctual and habitual. It did not feel abnormal. It's the nature of the art form to practice and rehearse for hours a day *looking into a mirror.* I was innocently laser-focused on the vehicle of my artistic expression: my body. This intense focus did not appear to be a problem, rather a focus that was required to succeed in the field of dance.

Given that my sense of self-worth was invisibly and mistakenly entwined with dance, I never entertained the option of *not* being a dancer. I did not initially question those feelings of unease when my body fell short in comparison to another. I took it as part of the game. An incentive to work harder.

But a seed had been planted in my mind: to ensure my sense of well-being and worthiness, I must conform and fit the mold. I began to restrict my food intake and slowly descend into the rabbit hole of dieting. By age 14, I had clear ideas and concepts about the kind of dancer I wanted to be: professional, respected and legitimate. For example, I was hurt and taken aback when a dance teacher made a passing comment that I would "probably do well in Las Vegas." [1] She meant it as a compliment, but I heard it as a letdown compared to the image of a dancer I had determined myself to be. Despite carrying her comment and the meaning I attached to it in the recesses of my mind, I persevered. After all, this was my self-worth, my passion and purpose; there was nothing else I wanted.

But the feelings of unease seemed to magnify when I happened to *not* be in the studio. When I was not dancing, I had the remaining hours of the day to grapple with painful insecurity and the bundle of thoughts that told me I *really wasn't* good enough.

In other words, I grew to expect to not feel so great when I was not engaged in my imagined source of well-being: dance. Understandably, that false belief began to form into a predictable low-level depression,

---

[1] In my young mind, I ignorantly assumed a showgirl in Las Vegas was not a respected and serious ambition in the field of dance. I felt it was a plan B of sorts for those not good enough to cut it. I know now that is not the case by any means. This just illustrates further the rigid and fixed image I had developed in my mind of who I should be.

always in the background, coupled with the endless scrutiny and comparison of my body but tolerated as if it was *just how life is, so you better pull yourself together.*

Between the ages of 15 and 17, I began to visit a lovely and well-intentioned therapist who gave me exercises and strategies to cope with the depression. One such exercise consisted of standing in the shower and imagining the water washing away all my negative thoughts and feelings. It sounded like a nice idea and I tried it, but then I had to eventually get of the shower. When I got out of the shower and the feelings returned, I assumed that I had not executed the strategy correctly. Back to the drawing board.

I continued with therapy and medication, finding respite in dance when I could, but ultimately I became incredibly discouraged by the notion that my feelings were to be continuously monitored and managed in order to prevent myself from being engulfed by them.

I bought into the cultural notion that having a greater percentage of good feelings meant I was *doing life right*, and having bad feelings was a sign that something was wrong with me and I needed to be fixed. That was not a life I wanted to live.

What I recognize now as my innate wisdom, but felt at the time like a desperate life-saving idea, guided me to propose the option of dropping out of high school during my sophomore year in order to train full time and pursue my passion.

My parents were understandably against this idea, and we settled on my attending an off-campus high school that enabled me to ultimately finish my remaining high school requirements in six months. I got my high school diploma at age 16. This was a remarkable opportunity for me because I was able to fast forward through high school and increase my dance training at the same time. Next up was my big dream: New York City.

The summer after I graduated from high school, I attended the summer dance intensive at New York University. I remember arriving at the hotel, looking out of the window at midtown Manhattan below and turning to my mother with a huge smile exclaiming, *"I'm home!"*

That summer cemented my love for the city that I had always held in my heart and I knew I had to return and move there for good. I auditioned for acceptance into NYU's Tisch School of the Arts dance department and was accepted for the term beginning in August 1993. With the incredible support and love of my family, I moved at age 18 to New York City.

This new adventure was going to be the answer to all my struggles and bad feelings.

Once again, I innocently connected my feelings to a circumstance and then innocently began to fall apart again.

My schedule at NYU was both grueling and wonderful. The training I was receiving was the best I could have hoped for, but my attempts to hold myself together began to get harder and harder. Toward the end of my first semester, I remember standing in dance class, utterly unable to look in the mirror and participate. I left in tears halfway through and returned to my dorm frantic to nip this pain of insecurity in the bud. I reached out to the university's mental health services and began seeing a psychologist again.

The woman I started therapy sessions with was a true New Yorker. I would visit her office on the Upper East Side, and she would chain smoke throughout our entire sessions-- I adored her! She was raw, honest and caring, and I always felt better when I left her office. I walked all the way back down to the East Village in wonder and amazement that I was living in this dream of a city. But the feelings came back again and again, with more intensity. My second year at NYU, I moved into my own apartment and still couldn't believe how amazing my life on the outside was.

Living and dancing in New York City was all I ever wanted.

So why did I still struggle with my feelings? Why hadn't the depression gone away if my dreams were coming true? What the hell was wrong with me?

It was these questions, and the confusion they spawned, that kept me suffering and looking for more ways to cope. More dieting, more restricting. Total obsession with my body kept me busy enough to distract from those painfully unanswerable questions. I didn't understand why my inner world of insecurity and fear did not match up with my circumstances, which were brilliant.

Enter full-on disordered eating, purging behaviors, and a triple pirouette of depression.

Despite my behaviors that I kept secret, I managed to graduate from NYU with honors and became artistic director of my own dance company. We rehearsed, performed, received grants and joined the illustrious downtown modern dance community. It was unbelievable.

I remember a striking and vivid feeling of being on the outside watching someone else's life and being dreadfully envious of it.

Since I believed my self-worth and sense of inner peace was so completely attributed to these *circumstances* -- my body, my career and my city -- it made complete sense to better manage, control, and do anything I could to keep the show running.

Obviously, that was an exhausting and impossible task, and trying to find my bearings in a fluid, naturally ever-changing outside world was tricky at best and utterly painful at worst.

It never occurred to me that perhaps my feelings never came from outside circumstances after all.

The misunderstanding of where I believed my good *or* bad feelings were coming from fostered an illusion that I proceeded to live inside: Dance and New York City gave me good feelings and self-worth, and I was not ok without them. As a result of this belief, I had to manage my imperfect body in order to be a worthy dancer and thus retain my well-being.

Living from this misunderstanding kept me blind to the obvious discrepancies and illogic inherent in that thought-created illusion: Sometimes I felt awful while dancing and sometimes I didn't. Sometimes I grew tired of the city and sometimes it was the most magical place on earth.

I did not yet make the connection that there *couldn't be a direct connection* between my feelings and my circumstances if I had different feeling states no matter where I was or what I was doing. It would be many years later before I would understand why it was so hard to feel better; I would *see* those destructive behaviors were but desperate tools attempting to sustain an illusion.

Trying to sustain an illusion is a never-ending rabbit hole.

Consequently, I found myself so deep in that rabbit hole that my health was on the line, and I decided to make a fearful move out of New York City -- the place that I believed held my heart and sense of self-worth. I moved to Austin, Texas, in 2001, where I entered into more regular psychotherapy and had family around to support what was a painful and disorienting transition.

During the next twelve years, I was a member of StillPoint Dance Company in Austin. Soon I eventually retired from dance-- discouraged by the fact that it was so difficult to untangle all the meaning and importance I had woven into it all those years. I continued to bounce between two poles: a false normalcy that involved sporadic occasions of eating-disordered behaviors (but constantly on guard, as they could strike at any time) and full-blown daily episodes of starve-binge-purge. Since I believed that there were such things as *triggers* (certain foods, situations, people), I had to avoid those as best I could. That meant my world shrank; my activities with others became severely limited, my routines that I deemed safe were strictly adhered to, and I had to isolate myself from a seemingly perilous outside world. I was still lost in an illusion that did not appear to be an illusion from the inside.

My only way out was to wake up.

For as long as I can remember, I have had an inkling that what we see in the visible world is not all there is. I was naturally drawn to seeking out and learning various esoteric and metaphysical teachings, devouring self-help books and following teachers and gurus who in my mind had the answers and knew the secrets that eluded me. The goal was to somehow by osmosis gain a sliver of understanding enough to end the search for relief from depression and catapult me into a grounded, stable, and safe place.

Looking back with what I've learned and experienced from this new understanding, I see that I innocently failed to realize that the peace, well-being, and resilience I was looking for were already inside me the entire time. There was no illusory place or state of mind to get to. I had studied and practiced yoga intensively in the year prior to leaving New York City and found the teachings of non-duality and *"you are not your thinking"* incredibly helpful. However, despite my total immersion in these ancient and powerful ideas, I did not yet have a solid grounding in which to sense the truth of them. They were only *good ideas* at that stage of my journey and so I remained deep inside my invisible cage, albeit now nicely decorated with Band-Aids of affirmations and mantras.

The principles that I write about and hope to point you towards in this book were what gave me a deeper understanding and grounding of what the wise and spiritual teachings have metaphorically pointed to for millennia, not to mention the relatively recent discoveries into quantum physics.

Innocently, we are taught to look outside, to circumstances and other people, for answers and guidance. As children, we automatically look to our caregivers to let us know what to do and when to do it. They know better; they teach us not to run into traffic, and how to feed and dress ourselves. While these lessons are incredibly important and valuable, what tends to trip us up is when we *continue* to look outside for answers and guidance, not knowing that perhaps we can trust, or that we even *have,* an innate GPS guidance system within. When we are suffering we inevitably look outside for answers and relief to stop the feeling of suffering. Perhaps that is why there is a huge and thriving self-help industry, feeding the hungry masses in our endless search for well-being. Huh.

Turns out those feelings of suffering and pain are built into us for a reason, a helpful reason. Those feelings that we don't like have been the victim of an innocent case of mistaken identity. You'll come to see why we've got it all backwards.

Turns out, we've been searching everywhere for the key to freedom that we've had all along.

That key is uncovered within this understanding.

TWO

The Missing Link

The beginning of knowledge is the discovery of something we do not understand.

-Frank Herbert

W illiam James, the American philosopher, physician, and later considered to be the father of modern psychology, wrote in the late nineteenth century that when the laws of psychology were discovered, they would impact humanity on a level akin to the discovery of fire. He wrote in 1892:

"[Psychology had] not a single law in the sense in which physics shows us laws, not a single proposition from which any consequence can casually be deducted .... The Galileo and the Lavoisier of psychology will be famous men indeed when they come, and come they someday surely will." (James)

It was in 2013 that I stumbled upon this understanding. I had googled *"how to stop bulimia"* and fortuitously came across a blog by Dr. Amy

Johnson, a psychologist who has since become a dear friend and colleague.

I instantly heard something very different in the way she talked about habits, addictions and being human, in general. I couldn't yet put my finger on why it was so different from what I heard in the past, but I always felt a sense of calm and relief when I read her blog posts.

I sensed something true on a deeper level than any therapeutic self-help material I had immersed myself in before. As I continued to follow her blog, I noticed a theme begin to emerge; a way of understanding that our habits and perceived problems didn't actually mean what we thought they meant. A way of understanding that was completely opposite to the *something-must-be-broken-and-needs-to-be-fixed* approach to mental health issues.

She had made reference to the Three Principles at one point, and I curiously googled it.

To be brutally honest, I was so entrenched and let down by all the other teachings, approaches, methods, and dogmas I had tried in the past that I dismissed what I had found on the web at that time about the Principles as yet another made-up cult of spirituality. But the *truth* that the Principles pointed to kept showing up and resonating with me in Amy's work and the works of others she often shared.

My curiosity was piqued again after several months when I realized everything that felt true and helpful *always* pointed back to these Principles, back to the *fact* that everyone has innate mental well-being; and I decided to go back and revisit for myself the origin and uncovering of the Three Principles.

To my surprise, the profound impact they had begun to make in pockets around the world was facilitated by many respected practitioners in the fields of both science and mental health. That gave me validation that what I was resonating with was not too good to be true and also carried a legitimacy that was worthy of further study.

Turns out the universal principles of which William James wrote were uncovered in 1972 by a ninth-grade-educated Scottish welder named Sydney Banks.

Banks was neither a spiritual seeker nor a religious man. He was riddled with insecurities and the afflictions of human suffering that seem like the normal resting state of people just trying to live their lives. I write about Banks not to tell his story, but to impart the huge significance of the fact that he was *not* a spiritual seeker climbing mountains in Tibet in search of enlightenment. He was just living his life as best he could. In other words, huge life-changing insights -- even "enlightenment" -- are available to *all* of us, not just the Buddha, et al.

While hiking in the mountains one weekend, he complained to a psychologist friend about how painful it was to be so insecure. The friend said something along the lines of, "Oh Syd, you're not insecure. You just *think* you are."

But he heard something in that statement on a *deep* level. On an insightful level.

This insight led to a remarkable enlightenment experience that upended his life and attracted psychologists, psychiatrists, medical doctors, and mystics from all over the world to come hear him speak on the small Island of Salt Spring in British Columbia. Soon he would even be invited to talk with physicists about this new understanding of the mind, as well as universities in B.C. and the United States.

He *saw* the principles behind our human psychological experience: he uncovered the *laws*, the missing link, what William James predicted would someday be uncovered.

I like to think that had James been alive today, he would be gratified that his prediction has indeed come to pass.

🌿

THREE

The Principles

Reality is merely an illusion, albeit a very persistent one.

-Albert Einstein

These three principles are descriptive, not prescriptive. In other words, they *explain* how our experience of life is created; they do not *prescribe* strategies or methods of *how* to live. For example, the principle of gravity does not tell us *how* to walk.

The English Cambridge Dictionary states a principle as:

A basic truth that explains or controls how something happens or works.

Why is this important to point out? When you know and understand *how* something works, you are not likely to devise strategies and coping mechanisms to help you deal with a seemingly mysterious phenomenon.

If we did not understand the principle of gravity, we would likely be horrified and confused every time we happen to trip and fall to the ground. Similarly, centuries ago humans thought illness was caused by bad smells; once we learned about germs, there was no reason to devise strategies in order to avoid and not be frightened of a nasty stench in the air lest it cause us to come down with the plague.

The same is true about the mind. When we understand insightfully *how* we are experiencing life, we no longer fear the *what* that may show up in any moment.

When I understood the fact **that** I think is immeasurably more important and profound than **what** I think in any moment, the content of my ever-changing mind loosened its grip on me.

The seemingly invasive thoughts of hating my body and worrying about food became more and more meaningless background static. It is that simple. Can you imagine?

Another fact that I find important to stress is that a principle is not a *belief*, *philosophy*, or a *good idea*; it is a *truth*. There is no wiggle room with a principle. And together, these three principles behind our human experience *only work one way*, as the definition suggests. This is good news. Why? Think about the principle of gravity again, if it was *not* a principle, if it only worked *some* of the time, that would cause us a lot of uncertainty in our everyday lives.

As you will hopefully come to see, if only *some* of our thoughts were untrue, which ones get that special place on the truth podium, and who decides?

Simply put, these are principles that govern psychology. They are spiritual in the sense that they are *formless*, so I will do my best to describe the formless in a way that I hope you can get a sense of, and not just an analytical understanding of. When first learning these principles many people can understand them intellectually, but then stop at that level and think "yeah, so what? How does this actually *help* me?" You might very well not understand the words at all, or you might compare these principles to other theories you've heard before. The difference is that these are *principles*, not theories—a principle is true whether we are aware of it or not. Gravity held us down to the earth before the principle of gravity was discovered and given a name.

Our intellect will obviously come into play when exploring something new, but try to look beyond the descriptions and notice the whisper of a feeling, a *knowing* you might sense behind the words. You'll find everything you need there. Don't try to understand with your intellect; just *listen*.

So, what are the Three Principles?

Mind, Thought, Consciousness

These are the basic, fundamental building blocks through which all our realities are created. They are presented as three descriptions, but it is **vital** to understand that they are essentially one. There cannot be an experience of life without *all three principles* working together as *one* compound. Furthermore, ultimately there is no separation between us and these principles; we *are* these principles in the same way that an ocean wave is a function of the ocean.

MIND

Mind, or *Universal* Mind, describes the intelligence that is behind -- and powers -- life. This is the impersonal, formless, constant and boundless energy of infinite potential. All form manifests from this formless Universal Mind.

 In other words, there is an *impersonal* intelligence that works behind the scenes to power life. It is this energy-before-form that spins the planets and beats hearts, an intelligence that is beyond human personal intelligence. It is what animates life; there is obviously *something* that distinguishes the living from the dead. It's the great mystery of the Universe.[2] Universal Mind is profoundly more vast than any religion. Religion is to Universal Mind as a thimble of water is to a vast, limitless ocean. One could say that Mind is analogous to the quantum field in science; a limitless, formless energy of pure potential.

Thought

Thought, or *Universal* Thought, is the energy with which we create our own realities, moment to moment. It is *impersonal*. It is not the *content* of our personal thinking, but it is the clay with which our personal thoughts are molded. Powered by Universal Mind, we then have the capacity to mold and create an infinitely vast array of new thought in each moment. The Principle of Thought is impersonal and unchanging, our personal thoughts created out of this energy are ever-changing throughout our entire lives.

---

[2] The word *God* has been so contaminated and manipulated by human kind that it holds limitations and concepts for many readers, so I refrain from correlating any God with my attempt to describe Universal Mind. Feel free to use any descriptor that resonates with you that points to the profundity of what 'Universal Mind' is.

Consciousness

Consciousness, or *Universal* Consciousness, is the principle that allows us to be *aware* of life. The principle of Consciousness is what's allowing you to be aware of the words you are reading right now. Consciousness brings the energy of Thought to life through our sensory system, it is what brings the *realness* to our *real*ities. It is the impersonal light of awareness that pervades and illuminates all experience.

Imagine an old-fashioned film projector. The film on the reel is **Thought**, the light that illuminates the film is **Consciousness**, and the electricity running through the power cord is **Mind**.

Another way of describing it is that we experience the enormous, formless potential of Mind via the brush strokes of Thought as a riveting and engaging reality brought to life via Consciousness.

What does this all mean? Simply put, our experience of life *only works one way:* **inside-out.** [3]

> *Thought creates our reality and then says, 'I didn't do it!'*
>
> *-David Bohm, theoretical physicist*

We *live* in the feeling of the energy of Thought in the moment, *not* in the feeling of our circumstances (the outside world). In other words,

---

[3] It is important to note that the phrase Inside-Out is not pointing to inside our bodies and minds (the form), but rather inside the Oneness of Mind, Consciousness, and Thought (the space within which forms are arising.) Both form and formless are ultimately One, i.e. of the same source. For the purposes of beginning to learn where our experience is being generated it's helpful to start with certain words and phrases as pointers that can later be transcended as understanding takes root.

we don't feel circumstances, we feel thought. One hundred percent of the time. No exceptions. It's an inside-out job.

The Three Principles describe how it is that I could have good feelings while dancing one day, and miserable feelings while dancing another day. It wasn't the activity that I was feeling, I was feeling the *thinking* I had in the moment. Another example is when we watch the same movie multiple times but have different feeling experiences each time. We aren't feeling the movie; we are feeling our thinking in that moment.

To be more specific, we are feeling the ebb and flow of the energy of Thought moment to moment and innocently attributing those feelings to our present circumstances.

Our experience moment to moment is only and ever inside-out.

It is really helpful to understand the fluid nature of thought. We *only* experience thought as it moves through moment to moment. A thought arises, we feel it, another thought arises, we feel it, and so on. Thoughts don't have a shelf life, they arise and are on their way out the moment we notice or *think* them. Then *poof* they are gone, with another thought following close behind.

Have you ever noticed that you can't actually have more than one thought at a time? Sometimes our thinking can be so split-second fast that it can feel like there is a jumble of noise in our head all at once. Consequently, that jumble is what we look at and listen to because it's loud, compelling, seductive, and looks meaningful—primarily because it's in our own head. Other times we have a relatively calm and quiet flow of thinking, which doesn't seem to pull us in and drag us around by the hair.

What if the fact that some thoughts feel more compelling than others meant absolutely nothing about what you are thinking *about?*

What if the loud, compelling thoughts had no more meaning and substance than the quiet, calm thoughts?

What if we only experience an ebb and flow of thought that changes costumes to play different roles in each moment but is ultimately the same substance underneath?

It is not only helpful but *vital* to understand that our feelings are not giving us information about *things*, i.e. circumstances, or people, but only information regarding the density, or volume of Thought energy we are experiencing in any moment.

We all have things that look like exceptions to the rule, things that don't look like thought (money, our partner, our jobs, our bodies, etc.), but those things can *only* be experienced via thought. And the nature of thought is fluid, changing, and arbitrary.

For example, I can feel anxious about my bank balance one day and secure and at ease the next day-- when the numbers haven't changed at all. Therefore, my bank balance *cannot* give me feelings. This is the logic of the Principles. This is the evidence of the inside-out nature of our lives.

I can feel fine and confident about my body in one moment, and insecure and frustrated the next moment. But my body hasn't changed in those moments, my thinking has. I have assumed that my body is giving me feelings that are telling me something about myself. But that is a misunderstanding.

When I was first learning the principles, I was at the gym one day and glanced in the mirror. Negative and hurtful thoughts popped up immediately as usual, but then something strange occurred to me. I had an insight. What if when I turned to look in the mirror the potential to have *any* thought applied to my body too. I saw in that moment that the silly thought "purple zebra sunshine" was just as random, arbitrary and meaningless as the thought "I'm fat." Woah.

Suddenly there was a pinprick-sized hole in the illusion of my thinking: I *saw* thought. Naked, without its costume of content and meaning.

I saw that *I* was creating the experience of unease by innocently believing random, habitual, untrue thoughts.

I *saw* how I was misunderstanding what thought was.

We can never directly experience the outside world. Our realities are created through the medium of Thought, brought to life by Consciousness, all powered by Universal Mind. Every human is subject to these same psychological principles, the content varies but the way in which the content is generated and thus experienced operates the same for everyone.

It only *looks* like we live our lives outside-in. It only looks like life is happening *to* us. Because of the magnificent *realness* that Consciousness brings to our thinking, it *really* looks like something outside of ourselves can give us feelings. This is the illusion.

But the *truth* is that we create what we experience (via Thought), and then we experience (via Consciousness) what we create.

We are *projecting* reality; we are not *receiving* it from the outside.

In other words, via the principles we use the creative medium of Thought *internally* to create our experience; our moment-to moment thinking, and then *feel* that thinking.

The correlation of what is happening in our circumstances and what feelings we have is just that: a correlation that is not even always evenly matched. Have you ever been driving and arrived at your destination only to realize that you missed the whole trip? If circumstances could give us thoughts and feelings, then we would only experience car-trip thoughts while in the car. But we don't.

If I am believing a thought that I have pre-judged to be not in line with who I think I am, I will *feel* that as anxiety, unease and insecurity--regardless of my circumstances.

For example, when I believe that my weight is an indicator of my self-worth, I will believe thoughts that look like evidence supporting that belief. And then I will *feel those thoughts* no matter what arbitrary number I happen to weigh. I will think that the anxiety is coming from the fact that I am the wrong weight. And the inverse: I will think my feelings of *okayness* are coming from the fact that I am the right weight.

THOUGHT = FEELING

In other words, a thought arises, gets "picked up" by consciousness and sent through my sensory system and thrown back at me as an experience of my weight. But it's not my weight I am experiencing, *it is thought*.

It's a 1:1 cause and effect that is entirely separate from circumstance.

Knowing through insightful experience that this 1:1 thought-feeling experience is only happening *internally* gives me a sense of relief from blaming and managing any outside circumstance that is ultimately always changing, and uncontrollable.

Notice how this is true for yourself, do your in-the-moment feelings *always*, 100 percent of the time match up to your circumstances? Why not? Do you think it's a fluke? Do you think you are an exception?

Have you overlooked the **fact** of Thought and Consciousness?

Could you consider the possibility that the prevailing outside-in nature of our experience **_isn't actually true?_**

That other people, our own bodies, our circumstances, or _anything_ outside of us isn't capable of producing our thought-feeling experience?

What would that mean for you in terms of your perceived struggles, problems, habits, and worries? What if you aren't an exception to the Principles behind every human being's experience?

I invite you to look in this direction—and keep looking.

I'm not asking you to adopt a new belief or add to an existing list of concepts. I'm not asking you to trust _me_, but to trust that there is something here to see. A trust akin to the way you trust that the sun will rise every morning.

The more you notice, the more is revealed.

✍

Glimpses of *Uncovery* from this chapter...

1. There are 3 formless principles behind our experience of life. They are descriptive and constant. These are the basic, fundamental building blocks through which all our realities are created.

2. Universal Mind describes the impersonal, formless, constant and boundless energy of infinite potential. All form manifests from this formless Universal Mind.

3. Universal Thought describes the energy with which we create our own realities, moment to moment. It is impersonal. It is not the content of our personal thinking, but it is the clay with which our personal thoughts are molded.

4. Universal Consciousness is the principle that allows us to be aware of life. It is what brings the realness to our realities. It is the impersonal light that illuminates all experience.

5. We *live* in the feeling of the energy of Thought in the moment, *not* in the feeling of our circumstances (the outside world). In other words, we don't feel circumstances, we feel thought. One hundred percent of the time.

6. We can never directly experience the outside world. Our realities are created through the medium of Thought, brought to life by Consciousness, all powered by Universal Mind.

7. The Principles are ONE, but are described in three ways for the purpose of beginning to understand and recognize our true nature.

FOUR

The Dance Between Illusion and Understanding

A circumstance cannot create your state of mind because a circumstance is a projection of your state of mind.

-Garett Kramer

Thought creates feeling, and in less than a split second, we believe that that feeling-experience is coming from something *other* than thought in the moment. This is the status – quo, outside-in misunderstanding of where our feelings are being created. Within this belief we then innocently blame, strive to change, praise, or become victim to circumstances and/or other people. But what gets us into trouble is *not knowing* that we are in this false belief. If I believe that my feelings are coming from my weight (or my job, or another person, and so on), I will obviously do what it takes to as-

ιy weight is where I think it should be to give me the feelings I think it is capable giving me. But it can't.

So I struggle and suffer, and I try to use strategies and coping skills to help me deal with the feelings (created by thought) of *struggle and suffering*. I will seek out the next best diet approach, the next grueling workout, and then end up starving and binging—then purging the food because my weight may go up if I don't (or so I *think*).

Now the eating disorder is the big problem to be tackled, instead of the root misunderstanding of where I believe my feelings are coming from.

Trying to control the perceived *outside* world in order to change my *inside* state of mind is the ultimate misunderstanding.

I am looking for feelings *outside* of where they are actually generated from. I am looking for security in an ever-changing, unpredictable, uncontrollable outside world. I'm trying to fix something that is *not the cause of my suffering*.

In other words, I am looking for security in people, things, my body, places, etc. that are always perceived differently by me *depending on the thinking I happen to have in the moment*. There is no security there.

Within the illusion (misunderstanding), I have innocently layered on piles of coping skills to deal with *failing* at *previous* coping skills. Now *those* coping skills look like the problem that I need to fix. But the fundamental misunderstanding is hiding *underneath* all of those layers.

The misunderstanding began when I innocently believed that my feelings were coming from **anything other than thought in the moment.** I believed that my body, where I lived, other people, and a million other things were giving me good or bad feelings. The *only* thing that creates feelings is thought in the moment. Only. Oh, and that re-al, solid-looking thing I'm thinking about? That's made of thought too: Money, My Body, Other People, My Job, etc.

We *live in what thinking feels like* moment to moment, it *is* our life. And here is the good news about seeing that insightfully:

The *very nature* of Thought is impermanent, impersonal, neutral, arbi-trary and always in flux moment to moment. That **fact** means that all I am *ever* up against is an ever-flowing, ever-changing, harmless **ener-gy**. I am *not* up against anything static or permanent or "real."

When I *see* the **fact** of this *in the moment*, it no longer makes sense to attach the cause of any given feeling to something in the outside world (including my body).

Engaging in behaviors that try to change, manage or control the out-side world doesn't make sense anymore when I know that those things are not the cause of my feelings.

I am not saying that things don't happen in the outside world, of course they do. What I am saying is that I can *only* experience those things through the filter of my own thinking—which is arbitrary, bias, and not a direct window on reality.

My eating-disordered behaviors began to fade away when I no longer needed an antidote to a poison that didn't exist. When I *saw* that I did not have to believe, or more importantly even *look* at, the content of my thoughts, I no longer had a wound to tend to. When I don't have a wound, it doesn't occur to me to use a bandage.

In the moments that I *don't* see it, I suffer, I struggle, I have feelings of frustration, anxiety and/or depression. I believe there is a wound to be healed. Treating a non-existent wound is fruitless and only leads to more frustration.

It is so important to point out that *nobody* lives 100 percent of the time *outside* of the illusion of thought. We literally live our lives in thought. The human experience is *designed* to be full, rich, and engaging. We are gifted via the Principles of Mind, Consciousness, and Thought with the ability to experience depths of feeling beyond measure. That unrelenting perception of the reality of our experience tends to also make it difficult to realize that it *is **not** real*.

> *Thought is not reality; yet it is through*
>
> *Thought that our realities*
>
> *are created.*
>
> *-Sydney Banks, The Missing Link*

But once you catch wise, even just a glimpse, to how it **only works one way**, you tend to wake up sooner out of the grips of a thought-storm. Everyone experiences thought-storms; hurricanes of intense thought that seem to have no clear exit for us. Before I learned about the nature of Thought, my thought storms looked something like this: "I can't believe I ate that---I'm so out-of-control—I'm going to gain weight—I need to throw-up—I will never get over this—what will I eat next—how do I know what to eat—am I hungry—should I try to distract myself—I need to just stop eating bad foods—I'm so hungry—I'm so full—I can't stand myself ..." And on and on; you get the picture.

When I did not know that the *only* thing I was feeling were these thoughts and *not* what my thoughts were *about* (because what the thoughts were about are made of thought, too), I was caught up in a storm, battered by the violent winds of panic. *I had no idea that what I was feeling had nothing to do with food or my body.*

This is a *radical* understanding to grasp.

Once you see your thoughts **AS** thought and nothing else, you have a fresh new moment to untangle any feelings from your innate well-being and worth.

It is interesting to note that if you ask people where they think their feelings are coming from, you will usually get one of three answers:

1. My feelings are coming from my circumstances and other people.
2. Sometimes my feelings are coming from my circumstances, and sometimes from my thoughts or moods.
3. My feelings are 100 percent generated from within the energy of Thought in the moment.

The logic of the Principles tells us that only number 3 is true. Since our experience of life is *only* generated from within, there cannot be an outside force that generates feeling.

Feelings in a thought-storm are not telling you *anything* except that you are experiencing a quality of thought that is untrustworthy and unreal. As you continue to see this for yourself—in the moment, the thought storms themselves begin to lose their charge.

They are revealed as the passing weather that they are. There is nothing to *do* about weather. And that's what you can rely on. We will *always* wake up; as thought continues to flow, our experience of it continues to change.

When I first came across the Principles, I started to notice the truth of them play out in every aspect of life. These little glimpses began to build my foundation of understanding and helped to prove the fact that once you see something from a deeply insightful level, you can never see it the old way again.

By way of example:

One day early on in my *uncovery*, I'm standing in Starbucks waiting for my coffee and I suddenly start to notice the other customers around me. There is a young couple, an older man, and a mother with her toddler, all standing in line with me. In an instant, I suddenly *see* them living in their thinking. I *see* how each one of us is having a completely *separate* inside-out experience of that coffee house.

Each one of us was creating our own experience of a circumstance. The older man at the end of the line seems agitated as he repeatedly looks down at his watch. The young couple are laughing at something on one of their phones and not paying attention to the queue moving on in front of them. The mother is trying to wrangle her toddler away from the display case. And then there is me, suddenly seeing clearly that I am experiencing *my* thinking—as if I have taken off a pair of cloudy glasses and can plainly see the Principles in action.

None of us are directly experiencing our circumstance, but **only** our thinking as it arises, moment to moment to moment.

We are all explorers in our own thought created experience of life. There is not LIFE over there, and Me over here experiencing it, rather I am creating and experiencing life via Mind, Thought and Consciousness moment to moment.

We all are.

🌿

Glimpses of *Uncovery* from this chapter...

1. Thought creates feeling, and in less than a split second, we believe that that feeling-experience is coming from something *other* than thought in the moment.

2. We *live in what thinking feels like* moment to moment, it *is* our life.

3. Trying to control the perceived *outside* world in order to change my *inside* state of mind is the ultimate misunderstanding.
I am looking for feelings *outside* of where they are actually generated from. I am looking for security in an ever-changing, unpredictable, uncontrollable outside world. I'm trying to fix something that is *not the cause of my suffering.*

4. Once you see thoughts **AS** thought and nothing else, you have a fresh new moment to untangle any feelings from your innate well-being and worth.

5. Life is not something separate from us, we *are* life... we are experience itself. Look for yourself, can you find a separate life outside of your experience?

FIVE

Looking In A New Direction

You're not afraid of what you think you're afraid of – you're afraid of what you think.

– Michael Neill

Imagine exploring life with an old-fashioned road map—the ones that are impossible to fold back up correctly (in my experience). Now, imagine one day you are so lost that you pull out your map and discover that there is a portion of the huge paper that you haven't unfolded all the way. All of a sudden there is a new route, a more direct path to where you are headed. A new direction to look towards. The Principles reveal this undiscovered direct route home.

By the time I began my introduction and exploration into the Principles, I had years upon years of cognitive behavioral therapy under my belt. (I had such a well-worn map that was so illegible with scribbles and notes that it never guided me anywhere new.) I did have periods of brief relief with this method, but I was always in a state of "waiting for the other shoe to drop."

I was in a perpetual state of looking over my shoulder, knowing that a relapse or trigger was trailing me from behind, just waiting for me to drop my guard. If I did not stay vigilant in my positive self-talk and constant re-framing of any thought that felt like it could do irreparable harm, I was in serious danger of teetering over the edge into self-destructive-behaviour-oblivion. (If I had a thought of "I hate my body" I was supposed to turn that thought into "I love my body, look at all thing good things it does, be grateful you even have a body" blah, blah, blah...)

I felt as if I was one chink in my armor away from bleeding out since I believed the constant manipulation of my thoughts from negative into positive was keeping me intact.

This self-imposed state of unease was rooted by the very method I was using to get *free* from unease. CBT is based on the belief that symptoms and associated distress can be reduced by teaching new information-processing skills and coping mechanisms. [Brewin 1996]

In other words, it is based on the very premise that thoughts are *inherently* harmful or helpful, and that the goal is to somehow neutralize the harmful ones and increase the helpful ones. All in the hopes of reducing unwanted behaviors.

The basic steps in a cognitive-behavioural assessment include:

Step 1: Identify critical behaviors
Step 2: Determine whether critical behaviors are
excessive or deficits

Step 3: Evaluate critical behaviors for frequency, duration, or intensity (obtain a baseline)
Step 4: If excess, attempt to decrease frequency, duration, or intensity
of behaviors; if deficits, attempt to increase behaviors. [Kaplan]

Notice the theme here? Behaviors.

This outside-in approach would make sense in the outside-in misunderstanding wherein we mistake our feelings and subsequent behaviors to be caused by outside circumstances.
As well as the misunderstanding that our thoughts are meaningful,
subject to control, and worthy of belief.
But we don't live an outside-in experience. That is the fundamental flaw
and the primary reason that a focus on behaviors and manipulating
our thinking does not transform people in a deep and sustainable
way. It simply cannot work that way because *we* don't work that way.
Focusing on my particular set of behaviors (the very first step in the
above assessment), starving-bingeing-purging, to try to stop them was
arduous, painful, and ultimately unsuccessful. The more I focused on
the behaviors (thinking about them, being afraid of them), the more
they were infused with an illusory power.
The more I tried to distract or white-knuckle my way through the
urges (*more* thinking about them), the more they were infused with
illusory power.
With all that imagined power and incredible amount of thinking, I felt
the heavy and constricted feelings that that thinking generated. (Because that's how it works: we feel our thinking.) And it felt *so* intense

that the only thing I saw to do was to relieve the pressure by engaging in the behaviors.

 Relapse. More thinking, more searching for a solution, and I looked again to therapy and professionals.

Within the old paradigm of psychology, I was guided to focus heavily on my urges and try to decipher them, looking for emotional significance and recognizing triggers and past causes. All this did for me was give thought meaning that thought just doesn't have. Thought is an energy. Flowing and transient and above all impersonal. (A huge relief to realize, which I will dive into in later chapters.)

Widely prescribed methods of resisting my urge (thought) to engage in my behavior were abundant, and not limited to journaling, bubble baths, calling a friend, and reading a book. All very nice things to do, except when the intention to do them was to control my urges.

Looking back, it seems so bizarre that taking a bubble bath would have any power to manipulate the ever-changing universal energy of Thought. (Which it didn't as you may have guessed.) But I wasn't yet awake to the nature of thought, (or the principles at all)—and neither were my therapists.

Without an insightful understanding of the Principles and an experience of *seeing* that we only ever live in thought—that **everything** is thought -- the best bubble bath in the world won't change a thing.

I remember an exercise where I wrote down a list of 100 alternative activities to do instead of my habit. One hundred! (I had to sit for a *long* time making up 100 random things to do.) So now I had a list of 100 ways to manipulate and trick myself into white-knuckling my way through a moment of unease.

Once in a while I chose one that worked, but it didn't work because of my made-up list. Unbeknownst to me it was simply because the natural flow of *thought* had changed, and I was having a different experience in the moment. *But it wasn't the activity that changed my thinking*, if that were the case, then that particular activity would have the same effect on my thinking all the time. Correlation is not causation. The list had nothing to do with it. The "better" activity had nothing to do with it. And that is why, even with 100 made-up alternatives, they never worked 100 percent of the time. That's not freedom. Real freedom is not bound by strategies that only work part time (or less).

Real freedom came when I realized *insightfully*-- through understanding the Principles behind my experience, that I did not need any strategies to feel better. Real freedom came when I realized the inside-out nature of my experience. Until I *saw* that truth, I was understandably discouraged that therapy was not helping.

This discouragement served to validate my false belief that this problem was permanent and would ultimately be a life-long struggle.

I was terrified of letting go of any techniques or methods (even if they didn't bring real freedom) because I was convinced that I was falling off a cliff if I wasn't using some sort of strategy in order to get better. I hadn't yet realized that the very intention of using a technique or strategy implied that the problem was expected to come back.

What I didn't yet *see* was that by leaping off the cliff, I would only be falling through, and ultimately landing in... Thought.

I simply did not see the role of Thought in my experience. I didn't yet realize that I would never stay in one feeling state permanently even if I wanted to; I had not yet been pointed in the direction of the **fact** of Thought and it's transient and impersonal nature.

In therapy, I had been guided to look at *what* I was thinking-- the content, the illusory stories, which was a never- ending rabbit hole.

In the absence of an understanding of the Principles, it seems as though addressing behaviors is the prudent strategy; however, the Principles point to the fact that behaviors are an *after-effect* of misunderstanding the arbitrary and impersonal nature of thought. In other words, behaviors are an attempt to change or control feelings because we believe that our feelings are coming from something other than transitory thought in the moment.

Attempts at changing or re-framing a thought are fruitless; it is akin to trying to sort out the separate ingredients of a cake *after* it has been baked. The point is, we *don't have to do that* because there is *always* thought moving through, moment to moment.

We *don't* need to go backwards and examine what arose the previous moment, as if it had a lasting life of its own. As if a thought meant something about us, our future, our past or our potential for change. The thoughts of shame and painful feelings that occurred after I had an eating-disordered episode were just as intense as the urges that led up to them. But I did not know they were simply the incredible creative energy of thought taking form in the moment, and not meaningful, true, or harmful to me.

The **fact** that we are *only and ever* living in the feeling of Thought in the moment and not *what* we are thinking about is incredibly liberating. The principle of Thought doesn't care **what** you are thinking, just like the principle of gravity doesn't care if you trip and fall. It's not telling you anything about **you.**

The *seeing* of the **fact** of Thought rather than **what** I think is the lasting game-changer that an understanding of the Principles gives us.

There is no real freedom in trying to manage our experience (i.e., our thinking and feeling in the moment). Attempts at managing an innately ever-changing experience of Thought is just not possible. **Or necessary.** It is looking in the wrong direction for change.

I was looking at the outside behaviors that were the result of me believing my thinking. I had so much real-looking *thinking* telling me that my body was the source of my self-worth that eventually that bundle of thoughts became a belief, and eventually that belief became an invisible background that I assumed was Me.

The Principles point us back to the source of our experience—the source from which any experience can and does arise. The space where the potential to think again, and again, lives. Everyone can sense that space, it is right here now, in the space between these words.

Since *all* thought and feeling is constantly changing and moving, **without our control**, it is a relief and a comfort to look towards what *doesn't* change or move: the vast space in which all my thoughts and feelings arise and wash away like an ocean.

I don't need to look towards what has *already* been created (a thought in the moment and a behavior in the next moment) when I can look *before* –to where *all thought* is created.

Looking in that direction automatically releases any grip or judgment I have on any unwanted thoughts.

They fall away back into the ocean, as waves naturally do.

Imagine how ridiculous it would be if the ocean picked out one momentary wave and said *this is Me.* That is what I was doing when I took a thought and believed it to be true. When I believed the thought that said *my body is not good enough* was true, I then automatically believed the next thought of *I don't like this truth, I must change it.*

How does the ocean change a wave?

Glimpses of *Uncovery* from this chapter...

1. Real freedom came when I realized *insightfully*-- through under-standing the Principles behind my experience, that I did not need any strategies to feel better.

2. Behaviors are an attempt to change or control feelings because we believe that our feelings are coming from something other than tran-sitory thought in the moment.

3. Since *all* thought and feeling is constantly changing and moving, *without our control*, it is a relief and a comfort to look towards what *doesn't* change or move: the vast space in which all my thoughts and feelings arise and wash away like an ocean.

SIX

What Is and What Isn't

*If we are open only to discoveries which will accord with what we know al-
ready, we may as well stay shut.*

—Alan Watts

One of the most helpful and profound truths we can understand and experience is that our thoughts and feelings
aren't ours.

We aren't creating our thoughts and feelings; they are arising within
us. For example, when I looked into the mirror and thought *'ugh, I
can't stand my body'* it wasn't me, *Amanda,* who created that thought
and the subsequent feeling it carried; it was me, *a human within which*
thought and feeling are experienced.

The Principles of Mind, Thought, and Consciousness describe how
those thoughts and feelings are being experienced *within* Amanda.
But Amanda does not create that phenomena herself.

That is an incredible relief.

Why?

Because I am off the hook from a futile attempt at creating the "right" thoughts and feelings, and I am off the hook from judging myself and going to battle against what is actually not personal at all.

Since those habitual thoughts feel real and feel like they are telling me about myself, not to mention they are in my voice and in my head, it is so easy to assume they are *mine*.

Not so. Impossible actually. And good news.

They are only "mine" in the (impersonal) sense that they are arising within me as I am a living, aware, thinking being.

When we innocently think our thoughts and feelings are personal, then they turn into a problem to be tackled, or a circumstance to blame, and generally something to fix. Or in the case of thoughts and feelings that we like and prefer, they become something we need to maintain. All because we have innocently mistaken that what goes through our heads is *ours*.

We claim possession of it all and hold ourselves responsible for those possessions, as if they have priceless value. Not realizing that they are all impermanent, changing, and impersonal phenomena.

What *is* real is our capacity to be aware of all the changing thought and feeling.

What *isn't* real are the thoughts, beliefs, stories, and judgments that appear and disappear and make up our experience of life.

What *isn't* real is my belief that my worth and well-being is conditional on the size and shape of my body, or what city I live in or what career I choose. What *isn't* real is the identity I create out of those beliefs.

What *is* real is the innate well-being that is ever present and untouchable.

What *is* real is the being that exists before all the beliefs and yet is also aware of those thoughts and beliefs.

Can you sense this for yourself? Can you start to see how we've got it all backwards; that our thoughts – ALL thoughts -- are not what is real, but what is real is the one who is aware of them?

When I began to *see* this truth, a funny thing happened: thoughts arose telling me that "it's not true, these thoughts *are* real and you'd better pay attention, or else!" I smiled and saw those thoughts for what they were too—not meaningful and nothing to attend to.

For me, when I *see* this in the moment I feel immediate calm and a sense of relief. I naturally dis-identify with all the directives, assumptions, and judgements. I naturally let go of trying to change and limit what is at nature always changing and limitless.

It's like the symphony stops playing and I can hear the soundless sound of the great opera house: silent, but with the soft rustling pages of a score being turned, and a quiet cough from the audience now and then.

I'm no longer following and interpreting every note I hear, yet I am aware of movement within the auditorium.

I know the symphony will begin another movement soon, but it's not a problem, because that's what symphonies do.

✄

Glimpses of *Uncovery* from this chapter...

1. We aren't creating our thoughts and feelings; they are arising within us.

2. When we innocently think our thoughts and feelings are personal, then they turn into a problem to be tackled, or a circumstance to blame, and generally something to fix.

3. What is real is our capacity to be aware of all the changing thought and feeling.

4. What *isn't* real are the thoughts, beliefs, stories, and judgments that appear and disappear and make up our experience of life.

5. When I see this truth in the moment, I naturally let go of trying to change and limit what is at nature always changing and limitless.

SEVEN

Icebergs in The Ocean

I am learning to see. I don't know why it is, but everything enters me more deeply and doesn't stop where it once used to. I have an interior that I never knew of...

—Rainer Maria Rilke

I magine the visible part of an iceberg above the surface of the ocean. That visible part was all my habitual thinking, feeling, starving, binging, and purging. The bigger unseen part of an iceberg is sometimes referred to as the keel. The keel is what directs the movement and shape of the top part, and which included all the thought that was invisible to me.

The Principles understanding works at the level of the keel.

By trying to change my thoughts, stop my purging, and manipulate my food intake, I was metaphorically taking a tiny chisel to the tip of the iceberg. Chip, chip, chipping away as best I could and not making any progress. No wonder.

If the keel determines the shape and direction of the tip of the iceberg, I was in a losing battle with my chisel. In other words, since I misunderstood where my experience was coming from; (thought in the moment) and those patterns of thought were invisible to me and were underlying my eating disorder, any change I was trying to make to the visible behavior was futile.

Letting go of my chisel was key. Understanding where the source of my experience was really coming from (under the water; within my understanding of the Principles of Mind, Thought, and Consciousness) began to warm the waters and dissolve the iceberg from the bottom up.

This meant that although the behaviors where still visible, the real change was occurring underneath—crumbling away and dissolving back into the surrounding water of awareness, and eventually the entire iceberg was gone; it was part of the ocean again.

Every time I found myself picking up the chisel again, the feeling of effort and struggle would arise, but through this understanding those feelings were now recognized as a really helpful feedback mechanism; reminding me to put down the chisel— those feelings do a good job of getting my attention. And that is what they are designed for, it's an amazingly effective system.

The following chapter will look more closely at just what those feelings are designed for.

❧

EIGHT

The Alarm of Wisdom

Urges are the buzz of your inner alarm clock.

-Dr Amy Johnson, The Little Book of Big Change

Remember that the Principles are *descriptive*, not prescriptive. They describe *how* our moment-to-moment experience of reality is created.

The Principles describe how my urges (thoughts) are brought to life, and how I get a full-on *real* feeling-experience of them. *Regardless of* **what** *those thoughts are.*

As I started to understand this deeper, what I began to notice was that the feelings that the urges (thoughts) carried felt familiar and habitual. The feelings of urgency and anxiety had a quality of familiarity that by definition I had felt before, but now I began to *notice* the familiarity.

In other words, I started to *see* the *familiarity* in a new insightful way. Instead of experiencing familiarity as a sign to expect the behaviors, I now began to experience familiarity as **all thought, too**. This new noticing of familiarity was uncovering the **fact** of thought behind the feelings that were invisibly leading me to starve, binge and purge.

The feelings had transformed *through insight* from being something to act on, to now being a wake-up call to the **fact** of thought creating my entire experience.

No longer were the urges an enemy to fight and subdue, but signals that were working in my best interest, like alarms that were a valuable guide to point me back to the power of Thought in the moment -- all to wake me up out of a thought storm.

Not to wake me up to look at the *content* and dig around in it while suffering the illusory meaning of thoughts, but to wake me up to the **fact** of thought. This is an important distinction: the content is ultimately meaningless and unimportant, because it's changing anyway. But the Principle of Thought *is* constant, and understanding this helps to point us back to what is really going on.

What was really going on to set off those signals?

Simple: I had loads of thinking in a moment that looked real and meaningful, carrying **intense** feeling with it, and my innate health (wisdom) sounded the alarm *to wake me up* and allow the system to untangle me from the illusion.

Before this insight, the urge-alarm was terrifying and felt like a weapon I very much needed to disarm before it harmed me. It felt as if I wanted to crawl out of my skin, that my head would explode if I didn't act on what felt like a call to battle.

In mainstream recovery, it is often suggested that one *sit* with an urge. (Remember my list of 100 alternatives-- my plan of action in case of emergency?) If I see the urge-alarm as a weapon pointed at me, it's incredibly hard, uncomfortable and generally unsuccessful to sit with it and stick a flower in the barrel.

I had innocently misunderstood what the alarm was in the first place. Within our innate health and wisdom, *there are no weapons.*

By realizing in any moment that I have a built-in system that has my back, I can let go of *fearing my fear of feelings.* Just that recognition alone clears the branches that block the river and allows the system of the Principles to more freely guide me back home.

Whether we understand or not, we will *always* reset to our factory settings at some point. (I was always going to survive an urge that felt like a weapon pointed at me.) It just happens with more ease and relief when you *do* have an understanding of how it works.

My urges kept signaling for a while during my exploration and learning curve inherent in understanding the Principles. **This is normal.**

It's like when you turn off a fan, the blades will keep spinning for a bit.

The habitual signals will catch up to the program and fall away as the understanding takes over the wheel. Sometimes I followed the urges, sometimes I didn't. But when I did, it felt different; it was more of a choice than a desperate act. Not that I was *choosing* to do harm to myself, but more of an acknowledgement that *in that moment* I was in an experience of the blades still spinning and I was doing my best with what thinking looked real to me.

The less I cared whether I followed an urge or not, the more they lessened in intensity. The change happens *underneath* the behaviors first, it transforms from the bottom-up, from inside to out.

We are gradually less afraid of the signals going off (because the signals are now understood for what they really are) and whether we engage in the behavior or not. The blades still spin for a bit.

It's not a problem.

It sounds counter intuitive, and people refer to it as "relapse," but I found that concept to be ultimately unhelpful, and points a shameful finger back toward the behavior. Not to mention the word 'relapse' has a gaggle of associations around it that are simply *just more thought*.

To be clear, I wasn't in denial or *"not getting better"* if I followed an urge at this stage of my *uncovery*, because I **knew** the change was happening at a deeper level and that the urges would catch up. And they did.

When we have that understanding, behaviors fall away, simply because there is nothing to cope with or fix. When the problem is no longer a problem, there is no need for a solution.

Sounds too simple, right? It *is* simple, and in fact it's *so* simple that we've missed it completely.

We are taught to be mindful, to pay attention to our thoughts, to *be present*. Without an understanding of the impersonal nature of Thought this is just another hollow piece of well-intentioned advice. It only serves to encourage us to *think about our thinking*. And there is no freedom to be found in that direction, only more confusion.

To begin to get a sense of why it's not helpful to analyze our thinking it may be helpful to make a distinction between *personal thinking* and the *Principle* of Thought.

Personal thinking can be seen as the content of our thoughts, the random musings going on inside our heads. The preferences, the fears, the worries, the commentary, the images of who we think we are and what we are capable of. When we focus on the *content* of our thinking, we get caught up in the stories and the imagined meanings attached to that content. A never-ending rabbit-hole.

In truth, those meanings are quite literally made-up and arbitrary. But they are in *our* heads, so we innocently believe they are real, that they are *us*. My thinking about my body, my career and where I lived became the story of Me. Innocently and completely 100 percent made-up.

The *Principle of Thought* is the impersonal energy that is the *source* of all our created personal thoughts. It is the clay that the content is sculpted out of.

When we can look away from the *content* of our thinking and recognize *that* we are thinking, we drop into a place of ease and lightness. We are no longer trying to block the river that naturally flows. New thought is *always* coming through, and with it the infinite possibility of a new experience in any moment.

A helpful metaphor is that of a grand apple tree. All the individual apples are our thoughts (lower case). Some are browning and bruised, some aren't quite ripe, some are beautiful and juicy and some are varying degrees in between. We innocently pick out certain apples, investigate them, banish them or indulge in their delicious flavor. The Principle of Thought (capital T), the creative energy, is the tree: the trunk, roots and branches. The tree is producing all these apples of varying quality.

It's incredibly freeing to stop looking at the individual apples and look toward what is creating them. New apples are always on their way; there is no need to fill your bucket and sort through any of them.

This distinction between our thinking and the Principle of Thought was helpful to me in the beginning, but in truth they are One. It's *all* Thought. And it's always in motion, ebbing and flowing. We cannot control what arises, or hold in place a particular thought. The very idea of doing so seems ridiculous when you catch a glimpse of the way the system works.

Let's take a deeper look at that system, and instead of taking my word for it, listen for what rings true for you. Explore what it's like to listen beyond the words, to a feeling that has no words attached to it.

❧

Glimpses of *Uncovery* from this chapter...

1. The Principles describe how my urges (thoughts) are brought to life, and how I get a full-on *real* feeling-experience of them. *Regardless of **what** those thoughts are.*

2. Instead of experiencing familiar and habitual thought/feelings as a sign to expect the behaviors, I now began to experience familiarity as *all thought, too.*

3. My urges kept signaling for a while during my exploration and learning curve inherent in understanding the Principles. This is normal.

4. When we have that understanding, behaviors fall away, simply because there is nothing to cope with or fix. When the problem is no longer a problem, there is no need for a solution.

5. When we can look away from the ***content*** of our thinking and recognize ***that*** we are thinking, we drop into a place of ease and lightness. We are no longer trying to block a river that naturally flows.

NINE

A Deeper Exploration

I very rarely think in words at all. A thought comes, and I may try to express it in words afterwards.

-Albert Einstein

A t first glance, it *appears* that things, people and circumstances have the ability to cause feelings in us. This is the basic outside-in misunderstanding that we have been conditioned in and have accepted without question. And accepted easily because it is seductive and convincing, and it *really looks like that's the way it is.* This old paradigm of how we think the mind works is steadily losing ground and being replaced with the new paradigm of the Three Principles understanding of innate health.[4]

---

[4] The term *innate health* is pointing to the fact of our true nature, what all great spiritual teachers for millennia have pointed to. We are whole, healthy, and complete *by nature.* There is nothing to fix but for the misunderstanding that we are *not* innately healthy. Just look at babies, they don't need strategies and affirmations to remind them of their true nature.

The new paradigm, the inside-out understanding of how the mind works, explains how, for example, two people can go to the same movie and have two completely different experiences, or how it is that we can have various feelings and/or reactions to the same circumstance when the circumstance hasn't changed. It explains why I can be annoyed in traffic one day and perfectly content to sit in traffic another day.

It's not the traffic, or any other circumstance or person that gives us good feelings or bad feelings.

Here is a breakdown of what is *actually* going on:

1. Thought Energy (the universal principle of Thought) is flowing through us at all times (whether or not we are having conscious thought). This energy carries what we experience as feelings.

2. Through the universal principle of Consciousness, we become *aware* of experiencing a feeling. It is brought to life as a full-on sensory experience.

3. The logical, higher brain attempts to search for a *cause* of this feeling and attaches it to something "outside," and now attributes that feeling to something *other than the energy of Thought in the moment.*

It goes without saying this all happens in the blink of an eye. We are constantly experiencing the feeling of Universal Thought energy, and we attribute feelings to something other than Thought. Our gift of personal thought colors our individual experiences and creates forms out of this energy. All internally.

What this all means is that we **only** experience life from the inside, out. The Principles are creating *through us* our moment-to-moment experience. This experience *is* our reality. There is no other reality for us.

Every single feeling, perception, and state of mind we experience is Thought coming to life within us, looking from our perspective like it's coming from the outside world. The "outside" also includes our bodies. When I have thoughts that my body is not good enough, or flawed, or what food to eat—I am not feeling those particular *things*—I am feeling my own thinking in the moment. But we don't see Thought, it's an invisible energy, we see the *things*.

(What's really amazing to realize is that those thoughts aren't even *mine*—I didn't create them to pop into my head.)

In essence, we *are* the Principles. Sometimes we can see it, sometimes we can't, but it is still the only way it works.

Sometimes we have a feeling that we can't nail down—we can't find a cause "out there" for why we are feeling the way we do in the moment. In these moments, our personal thinking will go on a search for a cause, and it's really up for grabs now. "Is it from the past? Is there something wrong with me? Why do I feel this way?"

When in fact, all that is happening is we are feeling the flow of Thought energy. Full stop. Not connected to any circumstance. Not personal.

> *Your mind goes where your thought goes, and once it goes there it justifies the thoughts that took it there.*
>
> Dr. Aaron Turner, One Thought Institute

Consider phobias for a moment. If someone has a fear of flying, they may have an intense, *real* feeling of panic before even boarding a plane (inside-out).

If it *were* the plane giving them feelings of panic (outside-in), they would need to physically be on the plane for that to be possible. Planes can't give us feelings.

The common phrase "it's all in your head" is thrown around as if that is explanation enough for someone to suddenly see through the illusion. But the illusion of thought is *so* convincing, so intimately woven into our very existence, that unless you begin to gain an understanding of the *fact* of thought and the fact of these Principles, you are unlikely to pierce the veil. However, there are many people who live a life of ease with no understanding of these principles. How? Because this is how we are made.

We are *designed* to bounce back and have new thought. It just happens to be incredibly helpful to have this understanding if you find yourself struggling and helplessly trying to mitigate that struggle.

How to begin to pierce the veil? It comes from insight. *A sight from within.* Insight is nothing more than a new, fresh thought. We've all had them. Some call them *Aha!* moments or epiphanies. When I suddenly *saw* that my urges were *only* thought-in-the-moment, and I didn't need to do anything with them or try to understand them or change them, or more importantly be afraid of them, that insight began to pierce the veil for me.

Insights allow us to *see* something new where suddenly everything is different, but nothing has changed.

Insights come with a feeling, a *knowing* that is obviously not coming from a database of old thinking. The most common and delightful insights I and the people I have worked with have had are ones that are not seemingly related to our "problem", but pierce the veil in a way that the "problem" suddenly doesn't look like a problem anymore. (I will share some of those examples from myself and my clients in a following chapter.)

You can't force an insight, you can't control what insights arise, but you can start to look in the direction of where insights come from. Out of the blue.

❧

Glimpses of *Uncovery* from this chapter...

1. We **only** experience life from the inside, out. The Principles are creating *through us* our moment-to-moment experience. This experience *is* our reality.

2. Every single feeling, perception, and state of mind we experience is Thought coming to life within us, looking like it's coming from a perceived outside world.

3. We don't see Thought, it's an invisible energy, we see *things*.

4. Insights allow us to *see* something new where suddenly everything is different, but nothing has changed.

TEN

Dragons and Shadows

> *No thought is really based in reality; reality is based in thought.*
>
> *-Michael Neill*

O ne of the pivotal insights I experienced came by way of a story told by Michael Neill, a transformative coach, author, and teacher of the Three Principles understanding. Insights can arise at any time, but often a simple metaphor or a story can be a powerful catalyst.

The interesting thing about insights is that they usually come when you are engaged in another activity, when your intellect is occupied with a simple task, like taking a shower or going on a walk. I happened to be cleaning house while I was listening and heard a deep truth, like a bright flash of light that brought what was once invisible into focus. With Michael's blessing, I share The Dragon Story with you here.

Imagine you lived in a world filled with evil, poisonous dragons. Nasty, fire-breathing, scratching, horrifying dragons. Naturally, living in that world, you would have to build up some pretty intense protection against the dragons. Some people would build their protective castle walls out of money; If they get enough money, the dragons won't be able to get them. Some people build their castle walls out of fame and success; if they can get famous and important enough, then the dragons won't get them. Some people use love to build their castle walls; if they can just get the right person to love them, then the dragons can't get them. Some build their castle wall out of perfection of body; if they are the right weight then the dragons can't get them.

And it sometimes, kind of, almost works ... until that person leaves them, or the money wall doesn't look so stable and now they are exposed. Or the fame starts to wane and those castle walls start to crumble. Or the body doesn't ever look right enough for long enough. At some point, you either give up on your castle, or your castle gives up on you, and life just doesn't work out the way you hoped. At that point, you get bit and scratched by the dragons, and it **hurts**. *It burns and tears through your bloodstream and it feels a lot like this thing they call stress. So the best you can do is take the edge off. Maybe you find that drinking helps remove the poison, maybe shopping distracts you from the poison. Maybe food and purging help dissolve the poison. We all have our favorite ways to deal with the dragon bites.*

Imagine all of that, and one day you wake up, to your amazement you realize, insightfully:

There. Are. No. Dragons.

That what looks like the shadow of a dragon on the wall, is really just a shadow of a thought. And you see people all around you running from the dragons, screaming in agony from the imagined dragon bites. Building their castles to protect themselves from the dragons. Sitting inside their castle walls in worlds that get smaller and smaller in order to feel safer and safer.

Now, you might still build castles, because castles are fun, but you wouldn't be building them out of desperation in order to keep the dragons out. And you would realize that what felt like dragon bites and poison was simply your own unrecognized thought. A transient energy that just comes and goes. Not a constant. Just shadows on the wall.

*When you don't drink the poison, you don't need the antidote. When you're not in a scary, mysterious discomfort that you don't know is already on its way out as your thinking changes, the behaviors will fall away by themselves. Because truthfully, **there are no dragons.***

I suddenly saw shadows upon shadows: layers of unrecognized thought all topped with a layer of visible behaviors that were ultimately not only sustained by shadows, but were shadows of thought themselves.

I saw that my eating disorder was not the dragon, but was only the salve I used to soothe the (imaginary) dragon bites.

This was something I had never considered. Not only was the eating disorder not the dragon, but the invisible belief I had been carrying around as Me-- that I had to be and look a certain way, and have a certain life in order to be worthy-- was the dragon... and that was not real, either!

I saw that the story was in essence only a bundle of thought that was so real to me that it turned into a belief, and then embedded itself into the background of my identity from which I tried to live from.

I was stunned. It was both disorienting and exhilarating. In the blink of an eye, I had seen through the veil of thinking I had been innocently believing for so many years.

I had no idea it was there, I only knew of the salve I was using to help with the dragon bites, because the salve (eating disorder) was visible. And what is visible is what we focus on and try to change, innocently. But since there are no dragons, I no longer needed any salve.

This insight was the spark that ignited my freedom.

ELEVEN

Understanding Insights

What you seek is seeking you.

-Rumi

It's helpful to understand what an insight really is: simply a *new* thought. And what we've seen about the nature of thought is that it is fleeting, temporary and *not real*. Insights will arise and are *specific for the moment*. In other words, the insight is not the truth, it's a portal that opens us up to *see* truth.

This is why trying to get the same impact out of a previous insight is impossible; it was new thought in a moment, and after that *sight from within*, it has been seen, and is no longer new. This is important to realize because we tend to think the specific insight is truth, but it was only a pointer; we need to look past it to the *truth it is pointing to.*

The insight I had about my eating disorder was not pointing to the eating disorder, it was pointing me to the fact of my invisible thought system. And even past that lies the truth of my innate health: that there is nothing wrong with me, and I don't need to do anything to prove my worth.

I hear this often from people I have coached: "I had this insight, but I can't get it back and now I doubt that I saw anything at all." The specific insight was the finger pointing them to truth and they were looking around for the finger. The truth they saw never went anywhere.

The good news is you don't need that same insight, because new thought is *always* **one thought away**.

Not one particular thought, but the recognition of *the flow of infinite possibilites of thought* where we are off the hook from the delusion that we can control or choose our thinking.

We don't have to chase an already flowing river of possibility.

Insight-chasing can be a common inclination once you have experienced an insight that shifted your foundation in a remarkable way. The fallacy is that the chase can easily morph into a strategy. We may start to ask, "How do I get more insights? What steps can I take?" There is literally nothing you need to do to summon an insight— because it arrives at exactly the right moment, and not before, with exactly the right information.

Again, the information insights provide are *pointing* to truth, they are form (thought) pointing to the formless essence (Mind) that is the fabric of our entire experience of life, and in which everything we are looking for is already here.

If this sounds too abstract and esoteric to you, that's ok—don't try to understand it with your intellect. You'll understand it through a *deeper seeing*—a sensed feeling, an insight.

The profound beauty of the Principles lies in the fact that we are already whole and well. Underneath all the chatter of thought, we are naturally habit-free and resilient. Insights point us further toward *seeing* and experiencing this innate health.

One of my favorite analogies around insights is when you go to a bookstore and buy a novel, you now have the entire book in your hands. But you can't *know* the entire story yet; you need to read it page by page, yet the whole *already exists*.

We are that whole novel, and insights guide us toward the truth, one page at a time.

❧

Glimpses of *Uncovery* from this chapter...

1. Insights will arise and are *specific for the moment*. In other words, the insight is not the truth, it's a portal that opens us up to *see* truth.

2. There is literally nothing you need to do to summon an insight— because it arrives at exactly the right moment, and not before, with exactly the right information.

3. Underneath all the chatter of thought, we are naturally habit-free and resilient. Insights point us further toward *seeing* and experiencing this innate health.

TWELVE

Connective Tissue Thoughts

> *Why do you stay in prison*
>
> *When the door is so wide open?*
>
> *-Rumi*

I had seen something deeply about the Principles and, in particular, around the principle of Thought. What I continued to learn is that even though we can *know* that we only experience Thought in the moment, that doesn't mean the principle of Consciousness isn't also at play. Remember the Principles are really *one*.

In other words, I will still *feel* my thought in the moment as **real** whether or not I've caught onto what's going on behind the scenes. The understanding may neutralize the intensity of the feelings, but if Thought is in play, feelings are in play. The Principles cannot be corralled or directed, only understood.

Ultimately, we learn that feeling any particular way is not a problem **or** a solution. It's the design. It is also built into the design to wake-up and realize when we have slid back into the outside-in misunderstanding of our experience. Included in that outside-in misunderstanding is the innocent belief that we need to feel better, or different at best, than we do in a particular moment.

The misunderstanding lies in the assumption that we need to *do* something in order to change our feeling state. We innocently think that we will be stuck in one feeling forever and it is up to us alone to *fix* that. We are seduced by the intensity of a feeling that we determine is unbearable, not knowing that *all* feeling is ultimately a transient, harmless energy. Just like we can't hold one particular thought in our heads for any significant length of time (try it!), we can't stay in the same feeling state even if we wanted to.

I saw this deeply while in conversation with Jacquie Forde, an insightful, fun and intuitive Principles Coach from Scotland who has been coaching and training others in this understanding for many years. Here is how the conversation unfolded:

AJ: I know this is just Thought, but I can't seem to see through it yet.

JF: Why do you need to see through it?

AJ: Because I want to feel better.

JF: Why do you need to feel better?

AJ: Um, uhh ... (them BOOM, it hit me) wait, I don't need to feel better!

Guess what happened? I felt better.

I suddenly *saw* that my wanting to feel better *was thought, too.*

I saw that no matter how well I understand the Principles, there will still be invisible thinking that may direct my moment-to-moment *visible* thinking. The feeling of frustration was my signal to wake up to the fact that there is something I am believing that is not true. In this case *I was believing that I needed to feel better.*

This ridiculously simple conversation brought this to light through insight-- from inside. I saw that in my trying and searching, I was feeling worse. The worse I felt about not feeling better, the harder I tried and the deeper I searched.

The relief came by remembering the truth about the ebb and flow of Thought in every moment, and that no feeling is permanent *or something to fix.*

It is interesting to notice that this was *not* the insight I thought I needed in order to feel better. I innocently assumed that I already knew the content of the insight that would lead to relief. I am still seeing this on a regular basis, but now it's a welcome and delightful curiosity.

> *When we pre-specify the insight we need, we stop looking for new thought.*
>
> *- Molly Gordon*

Ultimately, chasing insight and strategizing the Principles is like looking for your glasses while they are on your face. You are literally looking through the lens *to find* the lens that you want to look through.

We become waves looking for water.

All there is to *do* is to understand, and understand again in the next moment. Anything else is an endless chasing of shadows. During another conversation with Jacquie, I saw something deeply that was not expected. I was looking for a particular insight, but what I saw was infinitely more helpful:

AJ: *I feel like there is a door or a barrier between me and an insight I want to have about some thinking I'm coming up against again and again. It's like I'm at the bottom of a hole and slowly climbing a ladder rung by rung to the surface, but can't get through the door at the very top. I feel like if I can just break through that barrier I will make a huge leap!*

I continued to go on and on about how if I could just open that elusive door, there was a huge insight on the other side. It really looked like a doorway was the only thing between me and freedom from some habitual thinking. I really wanted to see past this particular thinking, I knew it was thought, but somehow clarity was being held captive behind this door that I couldn't find the key to. I needed an insight to unlock the door.

Then the unexpected happened.

JF: *Amanda, there is no door. There is no hole, no ladder, no rungs, no barrier, no key. There is Thought.*

Suddenly my eyes began to tear up and a feeling of beautiful relief overcame me. I saw it. I *saw the thinking* that was creating the illusion of a door between me and insight. *The door was thought*—and it was gone in an instant. There was no barrier--there was thought; there was no key needed because there was no lock.

It's kind of like suddenly seeing the connective tissue between major organs. The thinking that was invisible *('why can't I get an insight into this...')* was the connective tissue holding the visible, habitual thoughts in place. Once I *saw* that connective thought **as** thought, the "problem" thinking was allowed to flow on through. There was no more blood supply to keep it alive.

It was an incredible awakening to the power of the Principles to create what looks real out of what is an illusion. That habitual thinking that I saw as being held in place behind a door was only being held in place by the *thought* of a door. When *that* thought was revealed, all of it dissolved back into nothingness. The waves returned into the ocean.

Glimpses of *Uncovery* from this chapter...

1. Feeling any particular way is not a problem **or** a solution. It's the design. It is also built into the design to wake-up and realize when we have slid back into the outside-in misunderstanding of our experience.

2. We are seduced by the intensity of a feeling that we determine is unbearable, not knowing that *all* feeling is ultimately a transient, harmless energy.

3. The worse I felt about not feeling better, the harder I tried and the deeper I searched. The relief came by remembering the truth about the ebb and flow of Thought in every moment, and that no feeling is permanent *or something to fix.*

4. Ultimately, chasing insight and strategizing the Principles is like looking for your glasses while they are on your face. You are literally looking through the lens *to find* the lens that you want to look through.

We become waves looking for water.

THIRTEEN

Troubleshooting for Dummies

The Three Principles is not a self-improvement course, trying to improve what is. Rather, it is understanding the nature of what is."

- Dicken Bettinger

When you purchase a new appliance, computer, or anything that has the capacity to go faulty, it will usually come with a troubleshooting guide. You may also be familiar with the wildly popular *For Dummies* books that offer non-intimidating instruction and guidance for any number of topics.

The Principles gives us one incredibly simple troubleshooting suggestion for any and all psychological hiccups.

There is often a learning curve when first exploring the Principles behind our experience. Since we live in thought like a fish lives in water, it is a continuous waking up to the fact of thought and the fact that there are no exceptions to the Principles. This continuous waking up is kind of like being under water and then noticing some air bubbles—reminding you that you are under water. Our feelings of discomfort are those air bubbles, reminding us that we are experiencing Thought in the moment, nothing else.

My learning curve went something like this (and continues to):

It's all thought.

It's *all* thought!

Oh, it's ALL thought!

The absolute power of Thought is so enormous that we can somewhat grasp it, and at best continue to see it. I recently saw this in an insight surrounding the thought-feeling connection. I had been experiencing some habitual thoughts that brought with them uncomfortable feelings, but thanks to my understanding of the Principles, I wasn't too worried about not feeling so good when these thoughts appeared. That allowed two things to occur: First was the insight that I did not have to be so serious about the fact that I couldn't yet see these thoughts as Thought (and not real). That insight brought a breath of relief while I continued to experience the illusory thought-created stories and their accompanying ill feelings.

Secondly, I was able to feel the "bad" feelings and get curious to see more about this situation. When the serious judgmental thinking surrounding my inability to get insight dissolved, there was room for curiosity. I knew it was just thought, and the uncomfortable feeling that it brought was evidence that it wasn't truth, but knowing this wasn't quite piercing the veil yet.

What happened next was an insight, not into the story I thought I needed to see through and let go of, but an insight that transformed the story into just a story made of thought. Here is how it unfolded as best as I can articulate it[5]:

Habitual thoughts arose—I noticed them and had the thought, "This thinking brings a feeling I don't enjoy, I wonder if I can sense a pause between the thought and the subsequent feeling?"

It changed.

I didn't even experience the predicted feeling of the initial habitual thought because a new thought (in the form of that question) came through and that was what I then experienced.

In other words, the thought (insight) came in a nanosecond before the feeling, and it shifted my experience because I was now feeling the new thought.

I didn't even need an answer to my question (in the form of words)—it was answered by experiencing the feeling of the question.

Moment to moment, we feel our ever-changing thinking and literally have a whole different experience of feeling from the next thought.

When we are struggling with anything in our lives, the Principles provide a discriminator that we can use to help bring us insight, relief and ease in whatever we are up against, which is always and only ever a thought created experience. Not a thought created experience of something horrible, but a thought created experience. Period.

Since the paradigm of the Three Principles tells us that we are only ever experiencing our thought-created reality in any moment and not something in the outside world, the following inquiry is our trouble-shooter that fits absolutely *any* scenario:

"Where do I think my feelings are coming from in this moment?"

---

[5] It is difficult to articulate an insight that is felt at a level beyond words. Try to get a sense of what I am attempting to share with you in a way that feels more like a glimmer, as opposed to an intellectual effort to understand.

Just asking that question, even without trying to answer or figure it out can funnel us back into the truth.

If the answer is anything but *"thought in the moment,"* then we know we are caught in the illusion of thought being brought to life as a temporary reality.

It is vital to understand that thought is not an enemy to be controlled, managed, or feared-- but only understood. And more importantly, understanding that feelings are an incredibly valuable guide. Depression, upset, or negativity are not feelings telling us about our circumstances, but only that our thinking has veered off-road and we need to step back and not trust what we are seeing through our clouded lens.

The old guard of psychology would have us believe that these feelings are indications of a problem to be teased out and managed, overcome, or at the least, coped with.

Thought is simply a transient energy taking different forms. Just like clouds in the sky, the sky doesn't determine which shape the clouds should take, or which birds are allowed to fly through. The sky doesn't manage, cope or deny what shows up. The sky doesn't concern itself with the presence of a certain shape of cloud or the storm that may appear, it is simply a backdrop in which these things appear and disappear.

We are like the sky. The weather is our moment-to-moment thought-feeling experience, and it is *always* changing.

There is nothing wrong.

❦

Glimpses of *Uncovery* from this chapter...

1. There is often a learning curve when first exploring the Principles behind our experience. Since we live in thought like a fish lives in water, it is a continuous waking up to the fact of thought and the fact that there are no exceptions to the Principles, i.e. "yeah, I know it's thought...but this problem is *real!*"

2. Our feelings of discomfort are reminding us that we are experiencing Thought in the moment, nothing else.

3. When we are struggling with anything in our lives, the Principles provide a discriminator that we can use to help bring us insight into whatever we are up against, which is always and only ever a thought created experience. Not a thought created experience of something horrible, but a thought created experience. Period.

4. The Principles provide a discriminator that will allow us to wake up to the fact of thought in the moment: "Where do I think my feelings are coming from in this moment?"

5. Depression, upset, or negativity are not feelings telling us about our circumstances, but only that our thinking has veered off-road and we need to step back and not trust what we are seeing through our clouded lens.

6. Thought is simply a transient energy taking different forms. There is nothing wrong.

FOURTEEN

Mythical Demons

Your body does not eliminate poisons by knowing their names. To try to control fear or depression or boredom by calling them names is to resort to superstition of trust in curses and invocations.

-Alan Watts

I heard for many years that what I was struggling with and fighting against were my "inner demons." Sound familiar? Particularly in the eating disorder recovery world, it is suggested that one identifies their urges as *the monster,* or *the demon,* or *the jerk.* Although well intentioned as a way to separate oneself from these "voices" preaching unhealthy behaviors, this directive is still missing the mark.

Undoubtedly, *recognizing* the thoughts that tell us to engage in habits can be useful (though they are pretty recognizable already)—but giving them a fixed identity, let alone a negative one is giving validation to an illusion. One more dragon to slay.

Remember thoughts are not "things" or "entities." Thought is a neutral energy that passes through our awareness. That's all.

My experience with this demon-approach went something like this:

"Oh boy, here comes that damn monster again telling me to starve and then binge and throw up. Ugh, what have I done to create this demon? I'm going to give it a piece of my mind and tell it to shut up! Maybe if I get angry enough and mean enough I'll show it who's boss and it will scurry away and leave me alone."

What did this inner thought-dialog do to the "monster"?

It breathed life into it. It made it even more *real* to me, and then became an entity to resist. All this thought upon thought increased the pressure which is what that damn monster wanted in the first place: because it knew how to release the pressure: engage in the behaviors.

But there was no monster; there was thought.

There was no pressure; there was thought.

Understanding that *all* thought is the same—underneath the demon costume or the fairy godmother costume, is exponentially more helpful and freeing than playing a never- ending game of dress-up.

You don't have inner demons, you have thought that you resist and label as real and scary and threatening. But when you start to *see* the nature of what thought actually is, how it's brought to life, and where it comes from, you will naturally wake up in those moments of struggle and see what is really going on:

Nothing.

❧

Glimpses of *Uncovery* from this chapter...

1. Thoughts are not "things" or "entities." Thought is a neutral energy that passes through our awareness. That's all.

2. You don't have inner demons, you have thought that you identify as real and scary and threatening, which leads to resisting it, which results in suffering.

3. Understanding that *all* thought is the same—underneath the demon costume or the fairy godmother costume, is exponentially more helpful and freeing than playing a never- ending game of dress-up.

FIFTEEN

Getting Out of The Way

As you live deeper in the heart, the mirror gets clearer and cleaner.

-Rumi

When we are in a low mood, experiencing unease or discomfort, we have been led to believe that analysis is the way to feel better. Quite the opposite is true. In fact, we will innocently prolong our suffering by analysing low moods *within* a low mood. It's like trying to clean a dirty mirror with a dirty rag.

We think we must figure out this discomfort, because if it's in our head then *surely* it must warrant attention, right?

Wrong.

Here is an example of how it might play out:

I feel so bad right now, but why? It must be what happened earlier. Yes, it's because I ate too much. I always do that. If I could just control this, I would be so much happier. I'm going to figure out how to fix this eating problem. But it's been so hard before, I've already tried so many things to solve this problem. I feel like I'm never going to get over this, I feel like I'm not ever going to be free. Why is it so hard to just be happy?

And on and on the dialog and analysis continue. And the worse I feel. No wonder.

All of these thoughts that followed the noticing of *I feel so bad right now* are carrying the same quality of feeling. In a nanosecond, the thought-dialog begins; infused with the discomfort that the dialog is trying to navigate through and away from.

Trying to figure out *why* I feel bad is the spark that ignites the dialog. The very investigation into the feeling; where it came from, what caused it, how it can be prevented in the future, is being investigated from within the same momentary feeling state--and therefore prolonging itself.

What to do?

Understand that the feeling itself is not telling me *about* anything but the fact of thought in the moment; not any particular thought content, but the *energy of Thought* arising and creating feeling.

And feelings are all normal and all temporary.

When we get out of the way of the flow of this river of energy, the current of Mind is unobstructed and can continue flowing.

Here is the same example from above after insight and understanding:

I feel so bad right now.

Think about the tide coming in on a beach. The tide comes in, we feel it, it ebbs back into the ocean and sometimes leaves debris behind.

Seashells, seaweed, and refuse may be temporarily left on the beach but will soon be washed away as well.

It's all a normal and temporary flow that does not need our intervention. What a relief.

Glimpses of *Uncovery* from this chapter...

1. We innocently prolong our suffering by analysing low moods *within* a low mood. It's like trying to clean a dirty mirror with a dirty rag.

2. Understand that feelings themselves are not telling you *about* anything but the fact of thought in the moment; not any particular thought content, but the *energy of Thought* arising and creating feeling.

3. All feelings are a normal and temporary flow that do not need our intervention.

SIXTEEN

The How-To and What-To-Do

Do not meditate—be.

Do not think that you are—be.

Don't think about being—you are.

--Ramana Maharshi

Naturally when people are suffering and looking for a better way to live they ask "how do I do it?" *How* do understanding these principles help me overcome my habits, worries and problems? *How* do I feel better? *How* do I change? *What* do I do? I asked the same How and What-to-do questions. The answers may be at first unsatisfying and disappointing—but only to the intellectual mind. It's the intellectual mind that is asking these questions in the first place and while there is absolutely nothing wrong with that, I've found the *how's* and *what to do's* are themselves a rabbit hole that never ends.

The intellectual mind wants concise, practical steps to follow. When those steps are applied and no change happens, however, the how-to question rears its head once again.

But there *are* answers that cut out the middle man of methods, strategies and practices—that point directly to where the truth resides, and lasting change unfolds.

How do I change?

I understand again and again where my experience of life is really being generated from: inside. Only.

Moment to moment, I can remember that nobody and nothing outside can create my internal experience.

I begin to notice that what is called the "outside" can only ever be experienced inside *me*. That means the only thing I am ever up against is the thinking I have in the moment, which is always changing.

What I perceive as the outside is only my in-the-moment projection of the internal manifestation of thought.

I understand that change is happening already by way of the always changing, never static flow of thought. I understand that what appears real to me is just a hologram that when seen in another moment can dissolve and look completely different.

I don't have to take my experience so seriously; I can trust that my feelings will alert me to the fact that I am not seeing things as they really are in that moment. The more I look in this direction, the more I sense and experience the truth of it.

Then how do I change the "inside" to get a better experience?

I don't have to. I begin to understand how thought comes to life and is experienced as the reality I see through my eyes.

I understand that it is *not my job* to control, fix or change my thoughts and feelings. I understand that it is *not my job* to maintain a good feeling in every moment. I do not need to manage my experience of life— when I understand this, my experience automatically becomes lighter and more fluid.

I understand that underneath all thought storms is an ever-present, natural peace and well-being that needs no fixing or improving.

I understand that I am connected to the intelligence inherent throughout the entire universe. I know this by the simple fact that I am alive, aware, and creating my moment-to-moment reality via Thought.

What do I do when I feel bad, anxious, and depressed?
Nothing.

I understand that *all* feelings are normal, temporary and incredibly helpful to point me back to the fact that I have a bunch of thinking present that I have innocently believed to be true and meaningful. These feelings are my best friend and my guide to wake me up to the illusion of thought I have innocently mistaken for reality.

I understand that when I am experiencing these feelings they are not telling me about my life or circumstances (which are made of thought too), but only reflecting the temporary flavor of thought in my awareness.

If there is anything to do, it is to *not* trust my thinking in the moment and drop into my understanding of what is really going on.

I understand that feelings are not harmful or dangerous, but helpful and temporary. I understand that I no longer need to assume possession or attempt to decipher any thought or feeling. I see them pass through and therefore land me back at home-base.

How do I stop engaging in my habitual behaviors?

I stop trying to fix a behavior that is the after-effect of a misunderstanding of the nature of thought. I understand that behaviors are the physical manifestation of a futile and unnecessary attempt to change a feeling.

I understand that there is no need to fix a feeling. I see behaviors fall away on their own when they no longer have any purpose, when it no longer occurs to me that a behavior will give me security and well-being that I *already innately have*.

I know that even though a behavior is unwanted and obviously something I want to change, it is still not the direction to look in for lasting, real change.

Given the ever-changing nature of thought, I understand that I have a clean slate in every moment.

I know that a behavior is not telling me anything but the fact that I am experiencing my thinking as real in the moment and attempting to change it myself. This very understanding is what will dissolve the need for behaviors—from the inside-out.

How do I stop habitual thought patterns?

I begin to see the neutrality of *all* thought. I no longer label thoughts as habitual or not; I see that doing so only strengthens their illusory pull and substance.

I stop identifying certain thoughts as '*the habitual bad guys that need to be stopped*'. I start to see my thinking-in-the-moment in a softer focus, a blurred-around-the edges kind of way. I understand that I don't have to change, reframe, or banish any thoughts because Thought is an ever-changing, fundamentally neutral energy.

I begin to understand that when I am confused and frustrated, I am simply wearing a pair of muddy goggles. I am looking too hard, trying too hard to see from eyes that are obscured by confusing and frustrated *thought*.

When the mud inevitably washes away, I see clearly again and my experience changes.

When I get to *see* that my *in-the-moment* creation of reality is but a hologram, that hologram begins to shimmer and lose solidity. I see that a momentary holographic reality is nothing to be afraid of. I can relax, not take my thinking so seriously and experience the experience of whatever shows up for me.

I notice this natural return to clarity again and again and begin to trust and expect and then *know* that this is my innate resilience that is always present no matter what thinking I may be seduced by.

All of these answers are pointing to the same truth for all of us: you are innately well, innately resilient and there is nothing wrong with you. There never has been. You are so magnificent that you cannot be damaged *or* improved upon.

There is only understanding and understanding again in the next moment. Your feelings will alert you to when you are mistaking your internal projections as real, you don't need to constantly monitor or referee yourself.

You can play the game of life without any threat of damage to your built-in well-being and peace. You can do anything, achieve or not achieve anything, because your worth is not conditional upon what you do or any thoughts and feelings that appear in any moment. You can experience both highs and lows and know that neither touch your innate well-of-being. You are free.

You have always been what you are searching for.

Glimpses of *Uncovery* from this chapter...

1. The only thing I am ever up against is thinking arising in the moment, which is always changing. I don't have to take my experience so seriously; I can trust that my feelings will alert me to the fact that I am not seeing things as they really are in that moment.

2. I do not need to manage my experience of life—when I understand this, my experience automatically becomes lighter and more fluid. I understand that it is *not my job* to control, fix or change my thoughts and feelings.

3. I understand that feelings are not harmful or dangerous, but helpful and temporary. I understand that I no longer need to assume possession or attempt to decipher any thought or feeling. I see them pass through and therefore land me back at home-base.

4. I stop trying to fix a behavior that is the after-effect of a misunderstanding of the nature of thought. I understand that behaviors are the physical manifestation of a futile and unnecessary attempt to change a feeling.

5. I start to see my thinking-in-the-moment in a softer focus, a blurred-around-the edges kind of way. I understand that I don't have to change, reframe, or banish any thoughts because Thought is an ever-changing, fundamentally neutral energy.

6. You are innately well, innately resilient and there is nothing wrong with you. Your worth is not conditional upon what you do or any thoughts or feelings that appear in any moment. You are free.

SEVENTEEN

Stories of Uncovery

> *I want to unfold.*
>
> *I don't want to be folded anywhere,*
>
> *because where I am folded,*
>
> *there I am a lie."*
>
> —*Rainer Maria Rilke*

The following are stories of transformation through an understanding of the Principles shared with permission from people I have had the pleasure of working with. My continued intention is that you may hear something for yourself in their stories. I learn just as much from them as they do from our conversations together. The beauty of the Principles is that they are universal, therefore they are in play in all of us and can transform anyone who looks in this direction.

Elsa is a woman from Europe who reached out to me for some coaching after listening to my Uncovery radio interview. She had been struggling with binge eating and anxiety and we began to correspond by email and skype. She writes in one of her early emails what she is seeing about grasping this understanding:

Today I had some more space. I saw that I don't have to 'get it' in order to do it right. It was more like bathing myself in those words of what I remember of our conversation and the radio show and they sank deeper. I recognized the moment when I was about to jump on it, to 'get' it, which sends me into a great deal of thinking (I did this a lot in my life). But I sensed that whenever I did that things really slipped out of my hands and it got complicated.

Today I managed to not do more. To not grab it. And I trusted instead. It is kind of unbelievable to me that everything could be ok even though I did not do my best, or do all I could in order to deserve something good in return. But something tells me that maybe you could be right: that I really only have to get in contact with the understanding and listen.

I don´t know what has changed but this last week was different. I got back to feeling at home-base more often. I didn't try to 'get it' but only to be there. To let those feelings be around me. Since I heard your radio talk and especially what you wrote to me has let me find trust in that understanding. But I thought maybe it is better if I do not write about my thinking all day long but instead do what you recommended to me which is listening and going a little deeper. I wanted to share what has happened because I could really witness such a change. And then I felt I wanted to write to you and the second I got up – it shifted. I mean I do not remember what it was – but I saw through it. That it is really   only   thought.

And now... I mean I still have feelings, but now it is ok. And I am alone in my flat but I am okay with it just as it is. Nothing has changed but every-thing is different.

And I sit here with so much wonder. And do not know what to think or say.

Even while Elsa found it difficult to believe there was nothing she needed to do to start to experience a shift in her reality, she trusted that she had sensed something true about what she was learning.
She began to get insight into the normal fluctuations of thought and how her urges to binge where not a problem but an opportunity to point herself back to her innate wisdom. She writes:

I've learned that all experience is safe because it is all 100 percent thought--And today I think I saw something in this: that even an urge is wisdom. That all humanness is good and needs no improvement. And I saw that our filter; how we experience Mind via thought which is always changing ... as mercy. I used to see my urge as a flaw, a thought that leads me into trouble if left uncontrolled. Now I find this newfound trust (I am okay with what I feel even without knowing what to do) makes space for more wisdom to come in. And this helps me to get crea-tive and open when it comes to situations where I do not want to follow old habits. And this is huge. Totally new. Love!!

As Elsa started to see her urges as wisdom and not something to be frightened of, she began to relax in the midst of them and listen in a deeper way: she heard mercy in them. Mercy that was a gift; not an urge that was a flaw. A natural result of her seeing mercy was relaxation and space; out of which she had an opportunity to choose a different way forward where there was no choice visible to her before.

As we continued our correspondence, Elsa began to see how the Principles were showing up in all aspects of her life, which is only natural given the universal nature of them. We often seek out answers to specific problems (binge eating in her case) but soon realize with deeper exploration of the Principles that our entire lives can be transformed.

She writes of such an insight:

I saw deeply how I have a habit of 'building problems.' Sometimes (often) I make a problem of a situation, I combine things that would usually not show up at all and take it to extremes. And I did that as this is very common in my family.

I got the insight of a map. I am standing at a certain point and from there I can find my way to a solution (via my understanding of the Principles) or I can do my habit of "problem building" and make up stuff that is untrue and unlikely and make things so hard for myself that I give up on everything. This insight helped to bring clarity to what I could not grasp easily from my early learning of the 3 Principles. Often, I couldn't believe others who teach this understanding as I didn't trust that it would be okay. But then I saw this map insight as 'others have found a way to that place of clarity-- it is possible to get there, it is just that I do not know the specific way to a solution yet.' I was taking for granted that there is another way, and seeing that insightfully changed my attitude in an instant.

Elsa realized that her habit of building problems in order to find a solution to a problem was just a habit of thought, and never landed her where she wanted to be—at a solution. When she writes about making stuff up that is untrue and unlikely to the degree that she "makes things so hard on myself that I give up on everything," what was happening was she was feeling all that thought and it felt over-whelming and too much—the content that looked real and the im-mense build-up of thought-energy itself. No wonder she would want to give up.

Recognizing the role of Thought in our habits is the best and only path to further insight.

As we start to understand and bring to light how our hidden habits of thought are only illusory, different solutions become easier to see on our map. Even if she did not know the answers right off the bat, her understanding allowed her to relax and trust that what she needs to know will be revealed along the way.

Our innate wisdom shows up in the precise moment that we need it, we only need to set out on a path and let our wisdom course correct us along the way. This can show up as intuitive nudges or crystal clear, 180-degree direction changes.

Sarah is a young woman in her twenties who reached out to me for coaching around binge eating behaviors, fear of weight- gain as well as navigating the after-effects of a painful break-up. She writes in one of her early emails:

I guess where I'm stuck is that I feel like I am helpless sometimes, because at some moments, it feels like part of my brain just goes to sleep and my real self is nowhere to be found. It's kind of frustrating, I almost feel like I don't have the capacity to see a different way sometimes. Or if I do, then it's not until way later after I've already done the damage (of a binge). Do you know what I mean?

The following is my reply:

YES, I know exactly what you are describing. Here is what I've seen:

There is no real or false self; there is only awareness, which is our true nature.

(That's a biggie, sit with it!)

This is where words get kind of tricky in attempting to describe our innate well-being.

What happens when it feels like in those moments that "part of your brain shuts down" is that you are caught up in the reality of what your thinking is projecting onto the screen of Consciousness. You are now in the movie and it feels so real- then the movie changes and you "wake up" to the fact that there was a scary/bad movie playing.

The thing is, it's ALL thought; it's all generated from the same source. When you come to see this on a deeper level, you will catch wise sooner.

I know you want it to happen now, but you've got to trust that it is happening and it will change in ways that you can't see right now. You are in the beginning stages of Seeing what's really going on, you are in the exact place you need to be.

I know you want to stop the binges and they WILL stop when you recognize the power of thought in the moment and how you don't have to be afraid of getting caught up-- because you know what's going on. You know that Thought is playing a really big role and it looks real and seductive.

Please do not worry about your weight. I promise it will take care of itself as you continue to look in this direction.

I want to keep pointing you away from focusing on the behaviors (I know it's hard!!) and back to what's actually going on: Thought is largely invisible (until it's not!) and we get caught up in it temporarily. That's all.

And of course you can't see another way when you are caught up, that's how it works.

Again, you can trust that you will catch wise sooner, maybe not every time, but the momentum has started.

Don't try to use your intellect to "get it"; just sit with this new way of looking and let it simmer. And watch what unfolds, however small or seemingly insignificant.

It is quite common to feel hijacked in the midst of a behavior (a binge, a thought-storm, any habitual behavior) but that is simply still only a thought-experience. We get used to thinking that feels like "Me" and "not ME," but that distinction is an illusion. Pointing Sarah toward the fact that it is ALL thought helps to pull her out of the personal significance she (innocently) gives her thinking.

She writes next about anxiety and how she is starting to become aware of the role of Thought in her experience:

I'm 25 and I have a few fine lines that make me really insecure. So today I'm with my 21-year-old friend who's relaxed and outgoing and I just started feeling insecure. I felt this tense anxiety and I knew it was like being in a dream and it wasn't real, but it was still uncomfortable and I didn't know what to do with myself. So sometimes it will be like I know I'm caught up but I'm so in it and I don't know how to act at the time.

I guess there's really nothing to do in those moments.

And as for my eating, it has been normal the past two days but I still have a bunch of worries about what to eat next, etc. I think not worrying about the weight for now will help, and just using my common sense in judging how much is too much. Does that sound right?

Although she is becoming aware of being caught up in the movie of her thinking, she has yet to see that her 21-year-old friend is not causing her anxiety. Her insecure thoughts that look real is what she is experiencing.

I reply:

You've got it! (And it'll keep coming!)

Your example was a great one: you knew you were caught up, so there was a little space between you and the thought-created experience (movie).

Important: the thought-feeling connection is still happening all the time even when you know you are caught up. At this point, you are exactly right: there is nothing to do.

You'll find that the tension and uncomfortable-ness will dissolve pretty quickly because you Know what's going on.

Just like the principle of gravity, we will still fall down if we trip on the sidewalk every time; but we **know** how gravity works and so we don't get scared and anxious when it happens.

This is the same principle: when you understand how your experience is brought to life within you, you are no longer afraid of having any experience.

And yes, you can always rely on your common sense - it will navigate you better than any advice or "food plan". You'll know it's your common sense (wisdom) by the whisper of a calm feeling that arises.

Any worry, tension, and/or anxiety feelings are always and only a bunch of revved up personal thinking that **means nothing**. Phew!

As our sessions together progressed, I continued to point her in the direction of thought creating her experience, not outside circumstances. Repeatedly pointing in this direction is essential when our habitual thought systems are largely invisible to us, including the incessant outside-in misunderstanding that we have been conditioned in since birth. Sarah eventually began to *see* more and more the role of Thought in creating her feeling experience, and thus her experience of feelings changed. She writes:

This year, I have had many opportunities to see the principles working in my life. I went from binge eating/smoking on a daily basis to a rare occasion-- almost effortlessly. I went through a horrible breakup and lost someone that I truly loved but continue to see glimpses of the other side, and I had many new insecurities pop up that are slowly becoming easier to deal with.

One thing I have seen for myself throughout all of these experiences is just how powerful thought is. I don't think I realized the role it had in creating my feelings, and therefore, my experience of life. I used to think,

"Well, if I feel this strongly about something, it must be true," or "Obviously, I'm going to give in to this craving if it feels this bad."

Before my understanding of the principles, I couldn't imagine simply letting urges just be there. I didn't realize that an imaginary scenario created by my own thought could feel like it was actually happening. It doesn't feel like harmless energy being caused by my thinking when I'm experiencing the pain of rejection over my breakup, or I'm not liking what I'm seeing in the mirror. Actually, it is very real to me in the moment and can have an effect on my whole day if I let it.

Sometimes I don't realize I've been caught up in thought until after I have spent a significant amount of time worrying, crying, or stressing in some way. When my mind clears, I will either see the situation in some new, helpful way that I didn't before or the situation just doesn't have the same effect on me.

I don't think there is a way to not get caught up at all or avoid experiencing these thought storms, but I do think it is helpful just to know that storms always pass. If I can't see that it is just my thinking right away, I can trust that I will later and go about my day. Instead of indulging in my thought habits, I just know what is going on so that it doesn't have the same effect on me that it used to.

I used to think that if I just thought a certain way or followed some routine that the negative thoughts and feelings would disappear. I would get really frustrated that I had spent so much time reading self- help books and watching videos, yet I found myself stuck in the same thoughts or habit later that night. I began to realize that the less seriously I take these experiences that are only made of my own thinking, the more quickly they pass.

Then I have my clarity back and can deal with a situation (if I still feel the need to) more effectively. It doesn't mean the negative thoughts aren't there or that I no longer feel insecure, anxious, depressed, lonely, etc. I just have a bit more insight as to what is going on, and I don't feel the need to change my experience so much. After all, I couldn't keep it the same if I tried!

Sarah recognized the fact that anytime any thought comes into her consciousness, consciousness makes it look and feel absolutely real—and she gets a real experience of it—*and* she's creating it. She doesn't have to change her thoughts and/or judge them, she only needs to *recognize* **that** it is all thought, therefore not real, therefore an illusion. Thought recognition and how we create the illusion that thought is *anything* more than thought is one of the most powerful truths we can recognize for ourselves.

Feelings are shadows of thought. Some are grey, some are beautiful rainbow colors, but they are nonetheless shadows. Jackie was struggling with an intermittent depression where life just looked *"grey"* to her. As she started to see her thoughts as a river of ever-flowing energy of new thought coming down stream all the time, she began to recognize the power she was innocently placing on her feelings. She writes:

I've started to see how I was looking at the shadows of my habitual thoughts and making them more solid by my dislike of them. I had seen this in the past and not sure why I was doing this again...but one reason may be that it's just my habitual brain patterns showing up and that it's no big deal. The more I fight with them, the more solid they get, the more I let them flow on through the more fluid they seem. So, once I saw what I was doing (again) the whole experience of the grey shadows was more like a reminder that I was trying to fix stoppage by trying to stop it! Like "oh there's that grey feeling...just let it do what it wants to do...which is to flow on by". And the Knowing that fresh water is somewhere upstream helps me do that.

Jackie also had concerns about procrastination; and why doing things she disliked doing was so hard. She was starting to see a lot about the nature of Thought and the *content* of thought and wanted to see more regarding "procrastination" and her innate wisdom. She asks:

So, with procrastination just being another flavor of thinking, is every-thing we perceive all essentially thought? Is all personal thought basically "content"? The stuff our 5 senses bring into our awareness? Like right now I'm hearing thunder in the distance and flies buzzing around me, seeing my iPad, my fingers moving, the lake in the background, feeling the chair cushion, the breeze, the warmth of the sun, AND the word thoughts flowing through as I type, the inner pictures and feeling sensa-tions ...is it all "content"? And if so it's all just my particular unique kalei-doscope that Thought (big T) is lighting up? Is that why procrastination thoughts are the same as "getting things done" thoughts?

And my thinking thoughts about wishing my kaleidoscope had way more "getting things done" content than "procrastination" content ...that's more content/thought?

That does seem like a river choked with debris and plants and stuff. No wonder I procrastinate! This doesn't seem like wisdom though. I mean I can kind of see it from a higher vantage point that the system itself is wisdom in form...but I'm not liking this particular form much.

I replied with the following:

Yeah, the "getting things done" content and the "procrastination" content are all one: thought.

So is the "I'm not liking this" form of content.
If you can see the higher vantage point that the system itself is wisdom in form, then that system also must include all the other forms. **It's one system.**
Procrastination content in the moment... not a problem. Getting stuff done content in the moment, not a problem either. If the system itself is wisdom in form (it is) then the branches of that tree can only be wisdom as well.
Remember the impersonal nature of the system- if you can also see the thinking that says "I don't like this" as yet another branch of that tree, then those thoughts that look like "yours" can be revealed as arbitrary and impersonal as well. That higher vantage point is helpful to hang out in.

I wanted to point her in the direction that our entire experience is made of thought in the moment. Using the metaphor of wisdom as a tree, all the branches of thought that reach out are of the same essence. Some of those branches may flail about wildly and some may gently sway in a peaceful manner, but one branch is not better or worse or more important or less important; they are impersonal and part of one system of the energy of thought.

From the limited view of our thinking minds in any moment, we color the branches as being separate and either good or bad. Getting to a higher vantage point in order to see the whole tree as connected helps us view our preferences in a more neutral way.

During the writing of this book, the solar eclipse of 2017 occurred on August 21. Jackie wrote beautifully about her experience of viewing it and the insights that arose for her:

My sister and our teenage daughters drove down to see the solar eclipse...what an amazing experience! She lives in Minneapolis and our drive would have been 5 hours each way...that morphed into 6 hours on the way there and we were racing south to reach a patch of blue sky (felt like we were storm-chasers ha!) and the metaphors of weather, blue sky and our thinking were totally coming up and making me laugh as we careened down the (mostly empty by this point) interstate passing cops parked on the side of the road looking up through protective glasses and totally ignoring the traffic.

With minutes to spare we pulled into a parking lot, tumbled out of the vehicle and witnessed the most amazing natural event! I have to say that watching the moon completely block out the sun, and then the flaring of the diamond as it moved out of the way reminded me of how when things seem dark and hopeless, the sun is still there...and when our thinking shifts something beautiful happens, just like that solar diamond. An insight, just like that solar diamond bursting into view, can take our breath away. Then the sun comes back as before, and we are bathed in its Truth, and it feels so lovely.

And then within minutes the clouds rolled back in, we headed back home in major thunder showers and congested highways with construction, and a 5 hour drive turned into 9 hours and the metaphor just kept on making me smile...because I know the sun is still there behind all that weather...and before and beneath all my thinking.

So I think that whole experience has become a touchstone for me...when the dark and stormy weather seems to be lasting forever I just can't forget the Truth of the sun. And the sun is within me, no driving required.

Ps. While I was watching the eclipse my thinking quieted down almost completely and I was immersed in the magic of the experience...but before and after I found myself reflecting in the way I described above.

Jackie's insight was a beautiful real-world example of the metaphor that our innate, true Self is the sky and our thoughts and feelings are weather moving through. No matter the ferocity of the weather, the sky remains untouched and ever-present. No matter the ferocity and real-ness of our thought-created experience; our true well-being and innate health remains untouched and ever present. This is truth and it is always right here, right now.

Sally also had a beautiful insight around her innate health. After learning this understanding, insights keep penetrating at deeper and deeper levels and something that we've heard repeatedly can land when we least expect. She writes:

I realized that in this moment, in this "now," I was IN pure consciousness – not analyzing, judging, thinking about ... anything. Then it hit me that ... in this moment, I am healthy. I don't have a habit ...

NOT, "well I'm not wanting to eat anything now, but there's cookies in the kitchen and I'll probably eat them later" ... or any of a dozen thoughts that CAN go through my head.

I have heard about "our innate health" in many different ways, but this time it was personal. I was used to thinking of it as a concept that "Yes, we all have innate health" but I had never made it personal. But for that moment, I, ME, Sally, was in innate health and I SAW that. I simply can't make it sound as calm and peaceful as it was, and how WHOLE I felt in that moment.

There were no chinks of habits and judgments gouged out of the moment, no past identities and labels, just me ... being healthy ... with no habit.

What a revelation! And if I can see more of those moments during my life (and I know they are there), then I think that eventually the habit-filled Sally may have to take a back seat to the innately healthy one! You recently mentioned the "elusive obvious" and I like to think that my wisdom and peace seems elusive, but it's only that I'm not recognizing it.

I feel a little shell-shocked, because I'm sounding so serene, yet nothing "outside" has changed – I still am too heavy, and I am aware that there are homemade cookies in the kitchen. But for now, feeling that I am whole and healthy IN THIS MOMENT is more than enough!

One of my favorite insights she writes about here is this:

There were no chinks of habits and judgments gouged out of the moment, no past identities and labels, just me...

Sally experienced her true nature in that moment. Free of any added thought-created stories form the past or the future. This is the innate health within all of us, always present--a backdrop which we can rely on during those moments when there *are* a bunch of thought-stories grabbing for our attention.

The more we can look in the direction of our innate wellbeing, the less we worry about what happens in any experience of thought.

We don't have to try to be perfect all the time, because we are already perfect in how our experience is being brought to life in each moment. We can live more from this understanding and not get so worried and caught up in the petty details of *what* we are thinking, and instead realize with awe that we have a perfectly functioning creative potential *to think anything.*

EIGHTEEN

Surprise!

You are a function of what the whole universe is doing in the same way that a wave is a function of what the whole ocean is doing.

– Alan Watts

I thought I knew what being free was supposed to look like. I thought I knew how long it should take. I thought I knew a lot about myself.

I was pleasantly surprised to find out I was completely wrong. What I had made up to be acceptable and preferable about myself and my life fell comically short in light of what I came to see through this understanding.

When we have innocent attachment to how something should look and be, we miss the fact that it can be better than we could ever make up.

I thought freedom from my habits and unease would give me a slice of the proverbial pie, when in fact I uncovered the entire pie. To stretch the metaphor even further, I realized that I *was* the entire pie. So are you.

I thought freedom meant I would have stable and everlasting self-confidence.

Surprise!

I don't fear moments of insecurity, I know my moods shift as they will and I don't read anything into it. I see that I don't have to *think confidently*, rather confidence is part of my design no matter what I am thinking.

Low mood? No big deal. I know its temporary, and it passes through ever more gracefully as I live from this understanding. I know my feelings aren't giving me information about *anything* but the quality of thought I'm experiencing.

Freedom.

I thought freedom meant I would finally accept my body with its perceived flaws.

Surprise!

My experience of my body is as fluid as my thinking—since that's the only way I can experience it, I don't need to *accept* anything that has no solidity or permanence-- and is gone with the next thought showing up. I know my in-the-moment thoughts are not a window on reality, and any flaw I find is but a bias and arbitrary perception—and always changing.

Freedom.

I thought freedom meant I would be able to eat like everyone else.

Surprise!

I don't have to eat like *anybody* else. I can eat what I am inclined to eat in the moment and not think anything more about it.

Freedom.

I thought freedom meant I would learn a lasting way to cope with my problems.

Surprise!

I don't need to cope with a thought-created moment of unease. I have no possession of "problems"; I experience life as it moves through me and if I'm caught in a swirl of thought, I know my exit is up ahead when my mind settles naturally. I see that any coping I try to do only *strengthens* the illusion of a thought-created moment. There are no "problems"; there is thought-created experience. Only. Ever.

Freedom.

What does freedom look like to you? Could it be even better than that? The answer is an unequivocal *yes*.

The momentum of the entire Universe powers through us. We can't get it wrong, we can't mess it up. This isn't just a new-age, fluffy *idea*...This is what's true, this is what's on the menu.

Sense it. It's there in the quiet beneath the noise, and it's ready to be uncovered within you; within the one consciousness that *you* are within.

NINETEEN

Stay Tuned

> *Suffering is not the opposite of happiness; it is the veiling of happiness. It is a call from happiness itself, reminding us that we have mistaken our Self for an idea, an image or an object.*
>
> *-Rupert Spira*

My greatest hope for you, dear reader, is that you have heard something in this book that resonates at a level that at least sparks curiosity and at best uncovers the hope that lies in this understanding of the principles behind our experience of life.

To uncover these truths for yourself will change your life. You can't take my word for it though, you must look toward where I have attempted to point you. There is something to see, but you must first be looking. The best way to continue to uncover and bring to the surface your true innate freedom and well-being is to stay in the game.

Dr. George Pransky, a leading pioneer in the Three Principles understanding, shares a great example of this: If the players in a ball game want to change the score of a game, they don't stare at the scoreboard to change it; they get back in the game. In other words, it does no good to focus your attention so much on how you are doing moment to moment as an indicator of where you will end up.

Instead, realize that your changing moods are not indicative of how well or how poorly you are doing on your journey—whatever that journey may be, but are only indicative of the thinking you are in at the moment.

How is this helpful? It allows us to more easily see the bigger picture, regardless of our changing and moving states of mind.

When I can recognize the noise of thinking that feels habitual, familiar—and uncomfortable, I can tune into a different channel. A deeper channel that whispers to us all the time but gets drowned out with louder, habitual thoughts. That deeper place is where all of your inspiration, freedom, and peace lives.

See if you can start to notice that new channel. Don't be so quick to shuffle it aside for fear of losing your regular channels of thought. They'll still be there, they aren't a problem, and they aren't telling you any new useful information or guidance.

There is a deeper, more trustworthy place to tune into. You've sensed it before because it's been guiding you since birth. It's built in, it's your factory setting.

Allow your new understanding of how *all* human beings experience life to spark your own Uncovery.

> *Keep knocking, and the joy inside will eventually open a window and look out to see who's there.*
>
> *-Rumi*

❧

Epilogue

November 18, 2017

As I write this epilogue, I am on Salt Spring Island, British Columbia, the beautiful island where the truth behind life was revealed to Sydney Banks.

I can sense the wonder and magic of realizing the simple knowledge that lies within everyone in the Universe. I *See* that what I thought about myself was only an illusion created by the mind, yet within that illusion it was real.

Stepping outside of the illusion of thought—if only for a glimpse is the most incredible and profound feeling I have ever had.

Nothing I *thought* to be true about myself was real. I am as connected to the Oneness of the Universe as every atom, tree, human, animal, planet and star is.

There is nowhere to go to get back to myself, there is nothing to do to be more or less of myself.

The words to describe this waking up are insufficient and limiting.

I can only sense and feel what it means to be conscious within Consciousness.

I am suddenly seeing that thoughts don't have Consciousness, rather *Consciousness has thoughts*. My thoughts are arising in the *space* of Consciousness. It appears that thought fills up that space so fully that awareness disappears and thoughts are all that exist. I can now see that the *only* substance to my thoughts is the *Knowing* of them.

When I know that I live within creation of thought, that nothing is as it appears, something about that realization fills me with ease and peace. I'm not in control, it's not all on me, and I am free to have my experience because it's happening.

All the struggle, pain and illusion are perfect.

Every waking up is perfect.

They are One, and I am home.

What I am really saying is that you don't need to do anything, because if you see yourself in the correct way, you are all as much extraordinary phenomenon of nature as trees, clouds, the patterns in running water, the flickering of fire, the arrangement of the stars, and the form of a galaxy.

You are all just like that, and there is nothing wrong with you at all.

—Alan Watts

Works Cited

C, Brewin. "Theoretical foundations of cognitive-behavioral therapy for anxiety and depression." *Annual Review of Psychology*. n.d.

Cambridge Academic Content Dictionary. *Cambridge Dictionary*. web. 2017.

James, William. *Writings 1878-1899*. Print. New York: The Library of America, 2008.

Kaplan, Robert and Dennis Saccuzzo. *Psychological Testing*. Wadsworth, n.d.

Recommended Reading

Just a few of my favorites, in no particular order ...

The Little Book of Big Change: The No-Willpower Approach to Breaking Any Habit, by Dr Amy Johnson

The Inside-Out Revolution: The Only Thing You Need to Know to Change Your Life Forever, by Michael Neill

The Missing Link: Reflections on Philosophy and Spirit, by Sydney Banks

Being Human: Essays on Thoughtmares, Bouncing Back, and Your True Nature, by Dr Amy Johnson

Coming Home: Uncovering the Foundations of Psychological Well-Being, by Dicken Bettinger and Natasha Swerdloff

Somebody Should Have Told Us: Simple Truths for Living Well, by Jack Pransky, PhD

The Space Within: Finding Your Way Back Home, by Michael Neill

Beyond Beliefs: The Lost Teachings of Sydney Banks, by Linda Quiring

Mind Yoga: The Simple Solution to Stress That You've Never Heard Before, by Mary Schiller

Exquisite Mind: How Three Principles Transformed my Life and How They Can Transform Yours, by Terry Rubenstein

Seduced by Consciousness: A Life with The Three Principles, by Jack Pransky, PhD

The Joy Formula: The Simple Equation That Will Change Your Life, by Mary Schiller

The Peach Who Thought She Had to Be a Coconut: Profound Reflections on the Power of Thought and Innate Resilience, by Terry Rubenstein

The Path of No Resistance: Why Overcoming is Simpler than You Think, by Garret Kramer

The Relationship Handbook: A Simple Guide to Satisfying Relationships - Anniversary Edition, by George Pransky, PhD

Our True Identity ...Three Principles, by Elsie Spittle

Marriage (The Soul Centered Series Book 1), by Rohini Ross

Beyond Imagination: A New Reality Awaits, by Elsie Spittle

Right Now, by Steve Chandler

A Rich Man's Secret: An Amazing Formula for Success, by Ken Roberts

Second Chance, by Sydney Banks

The Enlightened Gardner, by Sydney Banks

More Resources

Websites and Practitioners

Amanda Jones

www.uncoveryspace.com

The Little School of Big Change

www.thelittleschoolofbigchange.com

Dr. Amy Johnson

www.dramyjohnson.com

Michael Neill

www.michaelneill.org

Jeanne Catherine Gray, Waking Up: The Neuroscience of Awareness

www.divineplay.com

Three Principles Global Community

www.3pgc.org

Sydney Banks materials

www.sydbanks.com

The Real Change Portal

www.realchange.info

Three Principles Movies
www.threeprinciplesmovies.com

Innate Health Centre, London
www.innatehealth.co

Jacquie Forde
www.jacquieforde.com

Pransky and Associates
www.pranskyandassociates.com

Rohini Ross
www.rohiniross.com

Molly Gordon, MCC
www.shaboominc.com

Three Principles Foundation
www.threeprinciplesfoundation.org

Barbara Patterson
www.barbarapatterson.com

Clare Dimond
www.claredimond.com

Judith A. Sedgeman, EdD

www.three-principles.com

Dicken Bettinger, Ed.D

www.3principlesmentoring.com

There are many more resources available to help you explore this understanding-- this is in no way an exhaustive list.

With my deepest love, I wish you happy exploring!

Acknowledgements

From the bottom of my heart I would like to thank the following people for their unending love, support, and inspiration before, during, and beyond the writing of this book:

My best friend and husband Danny Stipp, my parents Skip and Susan Jones, Abby, Fernando, Sofia, Antonio, Mario and Adrian Parra, Dr. Amy Johnson, Michael Neill, Jacquie Forde, Rohini Ross, Barb Patterson, Mary Schiller, Dicken Bettinger, Sandra Koenig, Bonnie Jarvis, Molly Gordon, Jeanne Catherine Gray, Elsie Spittle, Chip and Jan Chipman, Drs. Bill and Linda Pettit, and the late Sydney Banks.

Thank you to my clients and the students in The Little School of Big Change who shared their stories in this book; I am honored and grateful to be on this exploration with you.

ABOUT THE AUTHOR

Amanda Jones uncovered freedom after 23 years of eating disorders and depression through a revolutionary understanding of the human experience. After decades of traditional psychotherapy and endless healing modalities Amanda finally found truth in the simplicity of The Three Principles, the new paradigm that has unleashed healing and transformation across the globe. A former dancer with a BFA in Dance from New York University, she now coaches and shares with others who are struggling or who are simply curious about how an understanding of the Principles can transform lives. Amanda is currently partnering with Dr. Amy Johnson in The Little School of Big Change helping countless people wake up to their true nature and uncover lasting freedom without will-power or strategies. Contact Amanda at <u>uncoveryspace@gmail.com</u>

Made in the USA
Middletown, DE
03 November 2019